Hunting Rabbits and Hares

DATE DUE

MY 28 '91			
JE 4 '91			
JA 13 '94			

Hunting
Rabbits and Hares

*The Complete Guide to
North America's Favorite Small Game*

Richard P. Smith

Stackpole Books

Copyright © 1986 by Stackpole Books

Published by
STACKPOLE BOOKS
Cameron and Kelker Streets
P.O. Box 1831
Harrisburg, PA 17105

Photos by author unless otherwise credited.

Printed in the U.S.A.

Library of Congress Cataloging-in-Publication Data

Smith, Richard P., 1949–
    Hunting rabbits and hares.

    Bibliography: p.
    Includes index.
    1. Rabbit hunting — North America.   2. Hare hunting —
North America.   I. Title.
SK341.R2S65   1986   799.2′59322   85-26195
ISBN 0-8117-2056-X

For George, who was responsible for a great introduction to rabbit and hare hunting.

Contents

Acknowledgments

I would like to thank the many people who have contributed in some way to the contents of this book. First and foremost is my uncle, George Smith, who took me on my first rabbit and hare hunts, along with my brother Bruce. We've shared many more over the years since then. Lorraine and Craig, George's wife and son, have helped me obtain some of the photos in the book, too.

A big thanks to Kansas Fish and Game personnel, Mike Cox, Wayne Van Zwoll, Gene Brehm, and Rob Manes, who were a tremendous help in obtaining photos on a hunt there. Fred Bruins and Jack Burt in Ontario let me share a hunt for European hares. Thanks also to Craig Albright, who has studied Arctic hares in Newfoundland and provided me with research reports on Arctic and snowshoe hares, and provided photos of Arctic hares for this book. Brian Hearn deserves credit for taking those photos.

Others whose help I would like to acknowledge are Bud Oakland, Thayne Smith, Joe Dell, Greg Schmidt, Mike Hogan, Tom Cooley, Ron Spomer, Bruce Wood, Robert McDowell, Dan White, Jim Haveman, plus many others I've shared hunts with, and biologists across North America who took the time to answer my questions about rabbits and hares. Last, but not least, I want to thank Lucy, my wife, for her help and understanding. She printed most of the photos for this book and helped in many other ways.

9

Introduction

There are numerous books in print about deer hunting (one of which I wrote), because deer are the most popular big game animals in North America. Rabbits and hares rank as the most popular and abundant small game animals on the continent, so you would think they would be likewise honored with volumes directed toward hunters eager to learn more about the animals and how to hunt them. That hasn't been the case, however.

You have opened the first pages of the first book devoted entirely to rabbit and hare hunting, and I'm proud to be the author of it. Like so many other hunters, I started out with rabbits and hares. They are perfect game for the beginning hunter: they are both numerous and widely distributed; the opportunity to hunt them is terrific, courtesy of lengthy seasons; and they often provide plenty of action, which

is so important to boys, girls, and adults being introduced to hunting. The same attributes make rabbits and hares popular with experienced hunters, too.

I have always enjoyed hunts for rabbits and hares, and don't expect that to change. The enjoyment isn't solely a question of bagging rabbits or hares, although that certainly is part of it. Hunts for these game animals have served as perfect excuses for spending time afield with close friends and relatives (plus dogs), who look forward to the hunt as much as I do. Even when I'm alone, hunting still provides a wonderful excuse to spend time in the outdoors.

The times when few, if any, rabbits or hares were taken still proved satisfying, for I enjoy the chase regardless of the outcome and I enjoy being outdoors more than indoors. I've come to realize that hunting and killing aren't the same, and the latter isn't necessary for the former to be successful. I didn't always appreciate or understand that fact, as some of you reading this may not. That comes with time.

Rabbit and hare hunts have helped me understand hunting and why I enjoy it. The pursuit of bunnies has also made me a better hunter, not only for small game but also for big game, and it can do the same for you. That realization is why I'm excited about having written this book, perhaps to play a small part in starting others on the road I have followed as a hunter. It's a good road, but not always easy to follow. The information on these pages is intended to help you over some of the hills and around some of the bumps to make the traveling a little easier.

While the beginning hunter will benefit most from this book, there's plenty of information on the following pages that should be both helpful and interesting to experienced rabbit and hare hunters, too. All the species of rabbits and hares in North America are covered, including how to identify them and their respective ranges. Chapters on tularemia and population cycles include facts that all rabbit and hare hunters should know, and there are some hunting techniques discussed that you may not have tried. The appendix contains a listing of all 50 states and the Canadian provinces, including the species of rabbits and hares present in each, along with dates of most recent hunting seasons and more.

Happy hunting!

1

All About Rabbits

As far as some hunters are concerned, there are no hares in North America, only rabbits; the word "hare" is not in their vocabulary. According to their system of classification, if it's not a cottontail it's a jack rabbit, snow jack, or snowshoe rabbit. This is an oversimplification and simply isn't accurate.

It is occasionally acceptable to call hares "rabbits"; I do it sometimes myself. In this book the word "rabbit" may be used in a way meant to include hares or when referring to a species of hare. For the most part, however, I try to be accurate when referring to rabbits and hares.

Both critters do exist in the United States and Canada. Rabbits belong to one genus and hares another, and there are a number of species of each. Most rabbits and hares are different in size and appearance, although in some cases the differ-ences within each genus may be subtle, difficult for the average person to distin-guish. It isn't just their physical difference that separates rabbits from hares, though. They are also classified differently be-cause of their condition at birth.

Rabbits are born helpless (the scientific term is "altricial"), their eyes are closed at birth and they are naked, or nearly so. They are born in nests to help protect them from the elements and predators until they develop enough to fend for themselves.

There are actually eight major species of rabbits; some of them are distinctly dif-ferent and others can be difficult for the untrained eye to tell apart. Common names for the various species of rabbit are the eastern, New England, Nuttall's (mountain), Audubon (desert), brush, marsh, swamp, and pygmy.

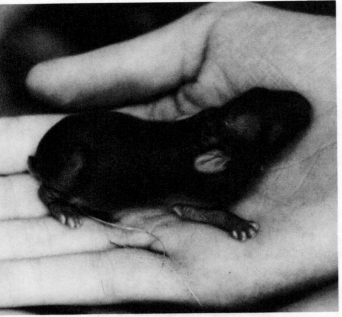

Rabbits are born helpless (altricial), blind and almost hairless.

Eastern cottontail are the most common and widespread rabbits in North America. They are found all across the eastern two-thirds of the United States and into southern portions of Ontario, Quebec, and Manitoba. Their range extends as far west as New Mexico and Arizona.

These highly adaptable critters are grayish-brown in color, with the nape of the neck rust-colored. Their bellies are white and feet are whitish. It's not unusual for eastern cottontails to have white spots on their foreheads. They range in weight between 2 and 4 pounds and are 15–18 inches in length.

Cottontails are known for their large white cottony tails that flash as they run. Tails of the eastern species vary from 1½ to about 3 inches in length. Ears are 2–2¾

inches long and hind feet 3½–4 inches in length.

These rabbits are prolific; an adult female is capable of producing up to seven litters a year, although the average is three or four. Litter sizes vary from one to nine young, with four or five per litter the overall average. Cottontail litter sizes average larger in the northern part of their range, where fewer litters are possible than in the south.

Dates when breeding begins vary, depending on latitude. The later spring arrives, the later breeding begins. An unusually late spring will delay breeding among cottontails, while an early one will have the opposite effect. Female cottontails in Texas, Louisiana, Mississippi, Alabama, and Oklahoma usually become impregnated for the first time from early to mid-February. However, one year during an early spring first conceptions were recorded on January 23 in Texas and January 20 in Louisiana. Breeding normally

White mark on this rabbit's forehead identifies it as an eastern cottontail, the most common and widespread species of rabbit in North America.

begins during late February and early March in states at latitudes between 35 and 40 degrees north, such as Tennessee, Kentucky, Missouri, Illinois, Kansas, and Colorado. At 40–45 degrees north latitude (Connecticut, New Hampshire, South Dakota, Minnesota, and Ontario) breeding among cottontails is delayed until late March or early April.

Baby cottontails are born after a gestation period that ranges between 28 and 32 days. Adult females become fertile again soon after giving birth and are often bred again. If not bred then, females will become fertile again in seven days.

Cottontail nests are often depressions in the ground lined and covered with grass and fur. Nurseries may also be in hollow logs and stumps, in burrows, or under brush piles. I recently saw a nest of newborn cottontails that was covered with a blanket of fur. The bodies of the tiny animals were black, and they appeared hairless. Their ears and feet were pink. Hair grows quickly on baby cottontails, so they aren't hairless for long. Their eyes open in about a week. The young leave the nest when between two and three weeks old, and they are weaned in their third or fourth week.

Female cottontails from first litters may become mothers themselves for the first time when five months old, although there are records of some conceiving at a younger age. Between 10 and 36 percent of juvenile females breed in their first year, depending on their physical condition, food supply, and location (how far north).

The size of home ranges of cottontails varies depending upon sex, quality of habitat, and the time of year, according to a Wisconsin study. From mid-March to mid-May, males were found to have an average home range of 6.8 acres. This

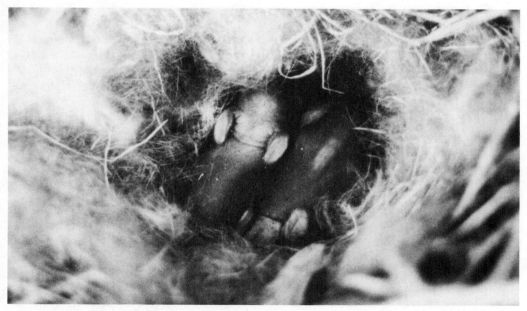

All rabbits are born in nests like these. The nests are usually lined and covered with the mother's hair or fur.

Top running speed of cottontails is about 20 miles an hour. This one was tagged as part of a California study. (Photo by California Department of Fish and Game)

went up to 9.9 acres from mid-May to mid-July, coinciding with the peak of the breeding season. The average home ranges of females were found to be largest during the period from March to May (4.3 acres) in conjunction with the onset of breeding activity. From May to July, the average size of home ranges declined to 2.1 acres as mothers cared for young. Home ranges were small for all cottontails during fall and winter months (September–January), with a spread from 0.7 to 4.2 acres and an average of 1.8 acres.

But there is more to know about eastern cottontails than mere statistics. Females, for example, average slightly larger than males. Like deer, male rabbits are referred to as bucks, and females as does; baby rabbits are called kittens. The potential lifespan of cottontails in captivity is nine or ten years, but those that reach five years of age in the wild are old-timers; from 70 to 85 percent of wild cottontails don't live to be one year old.

While researching this book I was surprised to learn that cottontails recycle their food at least once, when woody fibers are involved, to aid in digestion. Ruminants such as cows and deer regurgitate food from their stomach and "chew their cud." But in rabbits, the food passes entirely through the digestive system once and is reingested directly from the anus as soft pellets or a nonpelletized paste. The hard, dry pills or button-shaped pellets that we recognize as rabbit droppings are produced after the second trip through the digestive system. This process of reingesting partially digested food is referred to as "coprophagy."

The top running speed for cottontails is about 20 miles an hour. Their body temperature is higher than that of humans, averaging between 102 and 105 degrees Fahrenheit. Because of the positioning of their eyes, rabbits have a range of vision that covers almost 360 degrees.

Cottontails often make homes in abandoned burrows excavated by woodchucks, marmots, prairie dogs, and ground squirrels. They also occupy other sheltered locations such as hollow trees, abandoned cars and junk piles, old buildings, piles of wood, and brush piles.

Cottontails aren't generally vocal, except when caught by a predator or seriously injured. At these moments they sometimes emit a series of high-pitched screams. Hunters who wound rabbits will occasionally hear them make this sound when retrieving the animals.

Once when visiting my friend Duaine Lake at a wooded location I heard a rabbit scream nearby. Duaine and I immediately knew what it was, and we headed out on different courses to see what had caught the rabbit. Its continual screams directed us. As I came over a hill, I saw the weeds moving about 30 feet away, then the screaming stopped. A second or two later, a young cottontail with blood on its side appeared and came right by me, running awkwardly. It stopped briefly a couple of feet away, long enough for me to see the white diamond on the top of its head, identifying it as an eastern cottontail.

Apparently, the predator had released its prey when it heard us approach. Neither of us saw what it was, but we concluded that it was probably a weasel or mink (the incident happened along a lake). If the predator had been larger, like a fox or a hawk, we would have seen it. Also, in the time it took us to get to the scene, a larger animal or bird probably would have killed the rabbit and started to carry it off.

Cottontails can be found in a variety of habitat types, but they are generally creatures of the edge and can often be found where two types of habitat come together, such as the borders of fields and woods and along fencerows. They like to spend their days in thick patches of cover of any type, where they are hard to see and get at.

New England cottontails are brownish and sprinkled with black. They often have a black patch between their ears and a broad stripe on the outer edge of the ears. A black spot on the head is not foolproof evidence the cottontail is the New England species, though.

The vital statistics for New England cottontails are close to those listed for the eastern variety. A major difference between the two is that the range of New Englands is shrinking while it increases for easterns. This species is simply not as adaptable as its close cousin. However, they do possess a survival factor, according to researcher Robert McDowell in Connecticut, that enables them to hang on in some areas. McDowell believes the survival factor probably has something to do with the animal's metabolism, enabling it to adapt to colder climates than easterns.

McDowell said the range of the New England cottontail may shrink further, but he doesn't think they will become extinct. These rabbits are found in northeastern states, such as Maine, New Hampshire, and Vermont, and along the Allegheny Mountain range.

Nuttall's or mountain cottontails are grayish-brown with black-tipped ears that are 2⅛–2⅝ inches long and densely furred inside. Their tails are 1¾–2 inches long; the hind foot 3½–4 inches. Overall length is 13¾–15½ inches and they average between 1½ and 2½ pounds. Their range extends north–south from southern Alberta and Saskatchewan to northern Arizona and New Mexico, and east–west from parts of the western Dakotas into eastern Oregon.

Desert or Audubon cottontails look like easterns with big ears: 3–4 inches long. They are slightly larger than the mountain variety, weighing 2–3 pounds and measuring 13¾–16½ inches. Tails of these rabbits are at least as big as easterns, some-

Mountain cottontail feeding on high grass. Note black-tipped ears.

times bigger. Because of the climate they live in, desert cottontails often mate year-round, with an average of three young per litter. These rabbits have been known to climb trees with sloping trunks. They range from eastern Montana south to Mexico and from California east to Texas.

Brush rabbits are one of the smallest cottontails. They are reddish-brown mottled with black. Weights range from 1 to 3 pounds and they are 11–14¾ inches long. Ears are short and dark, measuring 1¾–2½ inches. Their legs are noticeably shorter than those of other cottontails, and their tails are small (¾–1¾ inches). Hind feet are 2½–3¼ inches long. Brush rabbits live along the West Coast from Oregon into Mexico.

The smallest rabbit isn't actually a cottontail because their tails aren't white, although they look like cottontails otherwise. *Pygmy rabbits* have gray tails measuring ¾–1¾ inches. Their bellies are a buff color rather than white like cotton-

tails. They also have whitish spots at the sides of nostrils.

Pygmies weigh 1 pound or less, are 9¾–11½ inches long, and have ears that measure 1½–2 inches long. Behaviorally, they dig their own burrows and are more vocal than cottontails. Preferred habitat is high sagebrush and greasewood. A maximum of three litters a year is born to does, averaging six young per litter; juvenile females generally don't breed. Their range includes southern Idaho, extreme southwest Montana, western Utah, much of Nevada, parts of eastern California, southeastern Washington and eastern Oregon.

Two types of rabbits are semiaquatic—marsh and swamp rabbits. The marsh variety is dark brown, except for the neck, which is cinnamon. Like the pygmy rabbit, this species does not have a white tail. Their small tail, measuring about 1½ inches, is grayish-brown on the underside.

Big-eared desert cottontail photographed in Arizona.

Marsh rabbits are semiaquatic, with short, wide ears. This one was photographed in Florida.

Marsh rabbits have short, broad ears that are 1½–2 inches long. Reddish-brown hind feet (the front feet are the same color) measure 3½ inches, body length is 14–18 inches, and their average weight is 3½ pounds. These rabbits are found along the East Coast from southeast Virginia to Florida.

Swamp rabbits rank as the biggest cottontails, weighing 3½–6 pounds and measuring 21 inches in length. They have a white tail, but it's thin, 2½–2¾ inches long. Their feet are rust-colored rather than whitish. Ears average 2½ inches in length.

There's another major difference between swampers and other cottontails.

Their gestation period is longer (38–40 days); the young are born furred and their eyes open soon after birth (within 2 or 3 days). This may be an adaptation for their aquatic environment. The range of swamp rabbits is from east Texas and Oklahoma to north Georgia and from north Arkansas to south Louisiana. There are also some in southern Illinois.

There is also one exotic (non-native) species of rabbit found in some parts of North America and on some islands in Hawaii: the *European or San Juan rabbit*. Although many of these are in captivity, some have been released in the wild, with sometimes disastrous results. These rab-

European rabbit sitting near entrance to burrow. These rabbits do a lot of digging and have become pests in some areas where they have been introduced.

bits are often brownish or grayish in color, but those in captivity vary greatly in color; all white, all black, and many combinations thereof are possible.

Brown European rabbits resemble cottontails, but are larger and have longer ears. They weigh 3–5 pounds and are as much as 2 feet in length. Their ears are 2½–4 inches long, tails 2½–3½ inches, and hind feet 3½–4½ inches. Tails are dark on top and white on the bottom.

European rabbits are good diggers, establishing a network of burrows (called warrens) with many entrances. A lighthouse keeper in the San Juan Islands, Washington, introduced some to his island. The rabbits did so much excavating that the lighthouse almost collapsed. Because of the damage, many of the animals were poisoned to reduce their numbers.

Other releases have been made on Middelm Island in Alaska, Farallon Islands in California, and on the mainland in Wisconsin, Illinois, New Jersey, Indiana, Maryland, and Pennsylvania. Other animals may have escaped from captivity in other locations. These imports are prolific. Does produce six litters or more per year, and each litter contains from four to twelve young.

2

Hares

Unlike rabbits, baby hares are precocial, meaning they are fully furred and their eyes are open at birth. Newborn hares are able to move about on their own almost immediately. Hares are generally larger than rabbits and have longer ears.

There are eight species of hares in North America, one of which is an exotic. Jack rabbits are actually not rabbits at all, but hares, and there are four species of them — black-tailed, white-tailed, antelope, and white-sided. Other hares are the snowshoe or varying hare, Arctic, tundra (northern), and European.

Snowshoes, the smallest hares, are actually similar in weight to eastern cottontails, but their bodies average a little longer. These hares weigh 2–4½ pounds and are 15–20½ inches long. Ears measure 3–4 inches, hind feet 4–6 inches, and tails 1–2 inches.

Snowshoes are sometimes called varying hares because they change color. During summer months, they have dark brown coats and their undersides are light-colored. The tops of tails are dark and bottoms are dusky to white. By late fall they become all white, with the exception of black-tipped ears. When molting from brown to white in the fall and white to brown in the spring, they are brownish-white or a mottled brown and white color. Their feet and ears change color first. This same characteristic is evident in other hares that change coat color, too.

The color change provides a natural camouflage, reducing the animal's visibility in its surroundings during the changing seasons. In western Washington, western Oregon, and southwestern British Columbia, where snow is uncommon, snowshoe hares remain brown all year. There is no

Snowshoe hares are the most common in the northern and mountain states, Canada, and Alaska. During summer months they are brown in color.

Snowshoe hare in winter coat of white, except for black-tipped ears.

Snowshoes (also called varying hares) change coat color from brown to white during late fall and from white to brown in the spring. This varying hare is in the process of molting.

need to change coat color for the winter, and the hares have adapted accordingly.

The range of snowshoe hares includes most of Canada and Alaska and extends southward along mountain ranges as far as California and northern New Mexico in the West and the Allegheny Mountains in the East. They also reside in northern portions of states bordering Canada and the Great Lakes such as North Dakota, Minnesota, Wisconsin, and Michigan, and they have been introduced in some other locations, too.

Like cottontails, female snowshoes are larger than males, and this is also true for other hares. Male hares are called bucks and females does. Baby hares are referred to as leverets.

Mature does produce two or three litters of young per year, with one to nine leverets per litter (average of three). Young will weigh 2½ ounces at birth, start to sample solids within a day or two, and are weaned within a month. The gestation period is 34–40 days. Does become fertile and can breed again after giving birth. Juvenile females from first litters of the year will occasionally produce litters of their own between mid-July and August.

Research has shown that average home ranges of snowshoe hares are 4–5 acres, but there is tremendous variation, depending on sex and age of the animals and time of year. Males roam over larger areas during periods of peak breeding, and juveniles may disperse up to 5 miles or more during the winter to move away from centers of high hare populations. Home ranges of varying hares don't normally exceed 20 acres.

Snow jacks have some interesting eating habits. They will eat meat or fish, especially during the winter, in addition to their normal diet of grass, leaves, and other green vegetation, twigs, and bark. As a result, they can be a nuisance to trappers using meat and fish as bait in sets. There are also reports of snowshoes, particularly females, eating sand or fine gravel during the breeding season. Like rabbits, showshoe hares recycle food through their digestive systems by practicing coprophagy.

These hares have been clocked at speeds up to 30 miles an hour. In the wild, varying hares seldom reach four or five years of age. They spend most of their time on the surface of the snow in thick cover, but will seek shelter under brush piles and blowdowns, and in hollow stumps and logs. They also will burrow into the snow, especially when it is deep and fluffy. Once I jumped a snowshoe that ran into an area where there wasn't much cover; it dived

Occasionally, an unusual snowshoe hare turns up. The black (melanistic) one on the right was bagged by John Vollner of Hancock, Michigan. His partner, Jim Gaspardo, shows a normal colored hare for comparison.

into the snow, then stuck its head up above the surface.

Like rabbits, showshoes, as well as other hares, are most vocal when caught by predators or injured. They make high-pitched screams. Commercial calls that imitate these screams are often used to lure fox, coyote, and bobcats to hunters.

Young aspen stands are good places to look for varying hares during both fall and winter, especially if heavy cover in the form of brush piles or a swamp is nearby. Favorite habitats during the winter, besides lowland evergreen and alder swamps, are thick stands of jack pines, even-aged spruce, and other pines planted as Christmas tree plantations or for timber. Most pine plantations are on private property, so be sure you have permission before hunting them.

Black-tailed jacks are gray, peppered with black on back and sides, and white on lower sides and belly. Two identifying characteristics are large ears and a black stripe on the tail that extends onto the rump. Ears are 6–7 inches long, brown with black tips. They radiate heat during hot weather; this helps keep the animals cool. Tails are 2–4½ inches long and hind feet measure 4½–6 inches. These jacks weigh 4–8 pounds and are 18–25 inches in overall length.

Blacktails don't turn white during winter months. In areas where the weather permits, blacktails breed year-round. Females produce from one to four litters per year, containing from one to eight young (usually two to four). Mothers place each leveret in a separate form or hiding place, to minimize losses; with this distribution, a predator may find one young hare, but not the others.

Speeds of 30–35 miles per hour are possible by these hares. When not running at top speed they will sometimes jump higher than normal at intervals to see better. Blacktails are capable of making 20-foot jumps horizontally.

Black-tailed hares are common in the western United States and also inhabit parts of the Midwest. Preferred habitat is open grassland, sagebrush, and desert shrubs. Blacktails have been found from California to Missouri plus Texas to southern South Dakota and southeastern Washington. Introductions of these hares have been made outside their normal range, too.

White-tailed jacks, as the name implies, have tails that are white on both top and bottom and are 2½–4½ inches long. They are brownish-gray during summer

Black-tailed jack hiding in shade of bush. (Photo by Gene Brehm, Kansas Fish and Game)

months, with ears that are gray on the front and whitish on the back with black stripes. Ears are 5–6 inches long. Whitetails become white with black-tipped ears during the winter, although in some areas they are a pale gray.

Weights range between 6 and 9½ pounds and they are 22–26 inches long. Hind feet are 5¾–7 inches. Each litter contains one to six young (four average), born after a 36–43-day gestation period. Whitetails have been clocked at speeds of 36–45 miles per hour and routinely go up on their hind legs periodically while running, for a better look around.

These hares tunnel into deep snow, sometimes excavating dirt in the process; soiled snow gives away the locations of whitetail burrows. White-tailed jacks can be found in farmland, grassland, and sagebrush flats. The range of jacks with white tails includes eastern Washington and Oregon and northeastern California to Minnesota, Iowa, and into Kansas. North to south, they extend from south-

White-tailed jack is the largest of the North American jacks. Some of them turn white during the winter, but this one is whitish-gray.

ern Alberta and Saskatchewan to Colorado and Utah.

Although white-tailed and black-tailed jacks are familiar to many hunters, antelope jacks are familiar to far fewer and white-sided jacks unknown to most. When researching this book I called the Arizona Department of Fish and Game to ask some questions about antelope jacks. The first agent I spoke to said there was no such animal!

One thing I want to make clear is that the antelope jack is *not* a jackalope. Jackalopes are the creation of imaginative taxidermists who combine the capes of real jacks with the antlers of small mule or white-tailed deer, to produce what has come to be known as a jackalope. There is no such thing in the wild. What puzzles me is why the concoctions are called jackalopes in the first place. I could understand it if pronghorn antelope horns were used. Since deer antlers are involved, a better name for them would be jackdeer.

There could be both black-tailed and white-tailed jackdeer.

At any rate, *antelope jacks* are similar to black-tailed jacks in appearance, but their range is much more limited in the United States. They are grayish-brown on the upper body, and their lower sides are white. The face, throat, and ears of these hares are brownish and the ears don't have black tips, but they are long (6–8 inches) and are edged in white. Tails are black on top, but this coloration doesn't extend onto the rump as with blacktails. The tails of antelope jacks are 2–3 inches long.

These hares weigh 6½–9½ pounds and are 21½–26 inches in length. Hind feet measure 5–6 inches. Antelope jacks flash their white sides as they run, when alarmed, to alert other hares. The sudden disappearance of white when the jacks stop is thought to confuse predators.

The only place antelope hares are found in the United States is south central Arizona. From there, their range extends

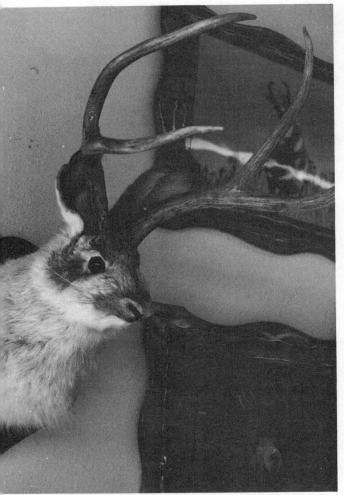

So-called jackalopes are the creations of taxidermists and do not occur in the wild. A better name for them would be jackdeer, since they are made with deer antlers.

south into Mexico. There were once thought to be some antelope jacks in southwestern New Mexico, but that population has proved to be the white-sided variety.

White-sided jacks are listed as an endangered species in the United States because of their scarcity. They are found only in the Animas and Playas valleys of southern Hidalgo County, New Mexico, near the Mexican border. From there the range extends southward into Mexico.

White-sided jacks resemble blacktails more than antelope jacks do. They both have black-topped tails and black-tipped ears. However, the ears of blacktails are tipped in black on the back sides and white on the front. White-sided jacks have the reverse: black tips on front and white on backs.

The endangered species also shows more white on flanks and sides when running than blacktails, and they are of a stockier build, too. A behavioral characteristic that separates the two species most of the time is that white-sides are most often observed in pairs. This rare hare is nocturnal, too, and found in desert grasslands.

Average litter size from a sample of ten female whitesided jacks is 2.2 young. They have been clocked at speeds in excess of 30 miles per hour. The hares leap straight in the air as high as 3 or 4 feet when disturbed, flashing the white on their sides as they kick with hind feet.

Male and female white-sided jacks collected in New Mexico by biologist Louise Kellogg in 1931 are housed at the Museum of Vertebrate Zoology in Berkeley, California.

The *Arctic hare* is the largest hare native to North America, weighing 6–15 pounds with an overall length of 19–27 inches. Hind feet are 5–7 inches, ears 2¾–3¼ inches, and tails 1½–3 inches.

Their bodies are gray–brown, with white bellies, tails, and backs of ears during the summer. They become white with black-tipped ears during winter months, like snowshoe hares. The hairs that make up winter coats of Arctic hares are white all the way to the base, whereas snowshoe hare hairs are gray at the base. Arctic hares on northern Baffin Island, Ellsmere Island, and Greenland remain white all year.

Female Arctic hares produce only one litter a year, consisting of four to eight young. They are born during late June or in July after a 50-day gestation period. The young are nursed for about two weeks, longer than other hares.

Their most common habitats are tundra and rocky slopes, although they will take shelter among trees, too, and they also burrow into the snow. Groups of 10–60 Arctic hares are not uncommon, especially in areas blown free of snow during the winter. Herds of Arctic hares numbering in the hundreds have been reported on some islands. When alarmed, these hares will sometimes stand erect and hop on toes of the hind feet, leaving tracks showing two footprints rather than four.

Newfoundland Arctic hare in winter coat of white with black-tipped ears. (Photo by Brian Hearn)

The range of these hares includes northern Canada from the Mackenzie River in the Northwest Territories eastward to Newfoundland. West of Hudson Bay they range as far south as northeastern Manitoba.

Tundra or northern hares are similar to Arctic hares, but their range includes only western and northern Alaska. In the summer they are reddish-brown or brown-gray in color. Their belly, legs, tail, and edge of ears are white, plus they exhibit white eye rings. Tundra hares become all white, except for black-tipped ears, for the winter.

They weigh 7–10 pounds, running a little lighter than Arctic hares. Body length is 22–27 inches. Hind feet are up to 7½ inches long, ears 3 inches and tails 2–4 inches. These hares are reported to make a "hoo-hoo" sound during the mating season. Other sounds they make (besides a scream when caught by a predator or

Arctic hare in summer coat. This one was photographed in Newfoundland by Brian Hearn.

injured) are described as huffing and hissing.

Although Arctic hares are the largest species native to North America, exotic European hares are now the largest on the continent. Weights up to 20 pounds have been reported, with small adults weighing 6½ pounds. They range between 25 and 27½ inches in length. Hind feet are 5–6 inches, ears 3–4 inches, and tails 2¾–4 inches.

Some of their features are similar to those of black-tailed jacks. Tails are black on top, but not the rump, and light on the bottom. The back of the ears is edged in black. However, these largest hares are brown with black hairs during the summer. They are gray-brown during the winter.

Three to four litters are born per year, containing anywhere from two to eight young (usually three to five), after a gestation period of 42–44 days. They are born in grass-lined forms, then the young are separated by their mother. Mothers use a buglelike call to assemble their young. They grate their teeth together as a warning sound.

These hares have been known to make bursts of speed up to 45 miles per hour, but 30 is more common. Jumps of five vertical feet to clear obstacles are easy for them. They are also good swimmers. European hares will tunnel into the snow for protection from the elements, but more often they occupy forms on the downwind sides of rocks, trees, fences, and snowdrifts. When abundant, they can do significant damage to apple trees.

Southern Ontario and portions of New York are where these hares are most abundant. They were first introduced in New York in 1893, when a wealthy resident of Dutchess County began importing them from Hungary in shipments of up to 500 each. Releases were continued until 1910 or 1911. In Ontario, European hares from Germany were released in 1912.

Mount of a European hare, the largest species of hare now on the continent. They were imported from Hungary and Germany. (Photo by Ontario Ministry of Natural Resources)

3

Rabbit and Hare Sign

Being able to identify and accurately interpret sign made by rabbits and hares is important to all hunters interested in these game animals, regardless of how they hunt.

The presence of tracks and other sign serves as hints to dog hunters about where to release their hounds. Knowledge about aging tracks will help hunters get hounds started on the freshest scent, and also enable them to help sort out the trail of a tricky bunny that has shaken a dog. Interpreting the freshness and direction of prints is a must for those who intend to trail their quarry in the snow on their own. Jump shooters and stand hunters who are able to interpret sign left by rabbits and hares can use this knowledge to choose the best locations to practice their chosen technique.

Tracks are the most common and readily identified type of sign made by rabbits

and hares. The track pattern is basically the same for all species. Prints from the four feet are grouped in a triangular shape. The triangle is actually formed by prints from three of the feet—the two hind feet are the base and one of the smaller front feet (frequently the right) is the apex. The other front footprint is often just inside the apex, but it can be lower.

Because of the way rabbits and hares move, front footprints are always *behind* prints made by hind feet in track patterns. So even if imprints from toes aren't visible, which they often aren't, it is possible to determine an animal's direction of travel. Rabbits and hares move in the direction *opposite* the way the imaginary triangle is pointed.

Tracks made by rabbits and hares are most distinct in the snow, but they can also be seen in soft sand or mud. Concen-

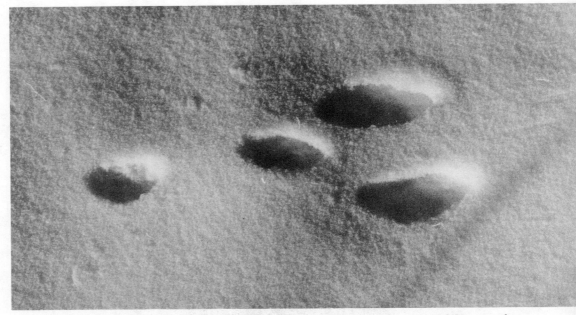

Tracks are the most commonly seen rabbit and hare sign. This triangular-shaped pattern was left by a snowshoe hare, moving left to right.

trations of tracks will be present in areas the animals frequent and where the critters are abundant. Bunnies will often pack down trails along routes they use on a regular basis, usually between bedding and feeding areas. Hares are notorious wanderers compared to rabbits, and so their trails often extend farther than those made by rabbits.

Aging tracks (determining how old they are) may seem difficult at first, but becomes easier with experience. Prevailing weather conditions actually have a lot to do with how easy or difficult it is to age tracks accurately. During a heavy snowfall, for example, tracks are quickly filled in and remain visible for only a short period of time. Any distinct rabbit or hare tracks seen under these conditions are sure to have been made only a short time before and can be considered fresh.

It's when there hasn't been any new snowfall for several days that aging tracks becomes tricky. Prints slowly start to fade soon after they are made and eventually disappear. Other than falling precipitation, wind and changing temperatures are the major factors that influence deterioration of tracks in the snow. Strong winds can wipe out tracks in the open as fast as heavy snow, and so can rapidly melting snow. With extremely cold temperatures, frost often forms in the bottom of old prints.

Wind and rain also affect the appearance and disappearance of tracks in the sand the same as they do in the snow. Strong wind or heavy rain usually wipes the slate clean. Wildlife of all kinds, including rabbits and hares, tend to be active after a storm of any type passes, and any tracks visible soon after the wind

Track pattern of a white-tailed jack rabbit when relaxed, in comparison to boot print.

Running track pattern of white-tailed jack. Notice that individual footprints are farther apart than in previous photo.

dies down or the rain stops are sure to be fresh.

The most important part of aging tracks is actually just a matter of distinguishing tracks that are most recently made from those that are older, whether they were laid down hours or days earlier. Fresh prints are normally the most distinct and show the most detail. Newly disturbed snow has a different character and appearance than flakes that were kicked up hours earlier, too.

I often check the freshness of tracks in the snow by comparing the detail evident in the prints with those left by my own feet. If there is a good comparison, the rabbit or hare tracks I'm looking at are probably fresh.

The distance between rear and front footprints, and the spacing between one "triangle" and the next, will usually tell you whether the animal was hopping at a normal relaxed pace, or was running. Track patterns of a relaxed snowshoe hare, for example, may measure 10–12 inches in length and the distance of hops is about 1 foot. When snowshoes jump into high gear, track patterns may be as much as 2 feet long and the distance between jumps as long as 6½ feet, as the animals make big jumps in their haste to change locations.

The hind feet of relaxed snowshoes leave prints that average 6 inches in length. In deep snow, the toes are usually spread to provide more support. Consequently, prints are widest at the front and narrowest at the heel.

Rear feet of eastern cottontails leave tracks that are normally 3–4 inches in length, and overall track patterns are 7–12 inches from front to back. Normal hops of these rabbits usually cover less than 1 foot. The smallest relative of the eastern

cottontail, the pygmy rabbit, leaves track patterns like the small rabbit it is: 6–7 inches deep at a relaxed pace, with hops of about 8 inches.

When both black-tailed and white-tailed jack rabbits are hopping, the entire length of the hind foot seldom leaves an imprint. Most of their weight often rests on only the front portion of these feet, and that's the only portion that leaves a track in the snow or sand. When they come to a stop and sit, though, the entire foot rests on the ground. Tracks from rear feet of whitetails measure about 3½ inches long when the animals are hopping and 6–7 inches when they put their entire foot down. Track patterns of these jacks can be 12–14 inches long, and they often make hops covering more than 1 foot. Subtract an inch from the measurements of hind footprints from whitetails and that's what blacktails should be, although there can be some overlap. Blacktails leave track patterns measuring between 9 and 12 inches and hop from 10 to 12 inches.

Both antelope and white-sided jacks are similar in size to blacktails. Arctic and European hares are similar in size to whitetails. The running track pattern of a European hare I jumped in Ontario was almost as long as my snowshoes. One hind footprint of a hopping hare was 5 inches long and the track pattern was 14 inches deep.

Joe Dell from Delmar, New York, sent me a photo of a running track pattern of another European hare that was almost as long as his pump shotgun.

Other types of sign that rabbits and hares leave besides tracks are droppings, feeding activity, and beds or forms. Droppings are in pellet form, resembling rounded pills or buttons in shape, but brown to green in color. These pellets are

Rabbit "buttons" or droppings compared to a dime. These were left by an eastern cottontail, but those of other rabbits and hares are similar.

ter, which boosted them up high enough to get at food that would have otherwise been out of their reach.

The bark of aspen trees is especially appealing to snowshoe hares, as well as other hares and rabbits, but they will nibble on a variety of other saplings and shrubs, too. Light-colored inner wood

similar for all rabbits and hares, with some slight variations in size. Accumulations of droppings are frequently present at favored feeding sites and forms.

Both rabbits and hares feed on plants, woody stems, twigs, and bark during the fall and winter. The animals' sharp incisor teeth (the big ones in front) enable them to nip food items off cleanly, but the cut isn't straight: stems and twigs are bitten off at an angle. Neat, angular cuts are unmistakable evidence that rabbits or hares have been dining.

Deer feed on similar food, but they lack teeth in the front of their mouths on top; they break twigs off, leaving a rough, ragged edge. Deer also feed on items higher off the ground than most rabbits or hares can reach. Evidence of browsing by hares or rabbits, however, may be noticed much higher off the ground than it would seem possible they could reach. The answer lies in the depth of the snow the previous win-

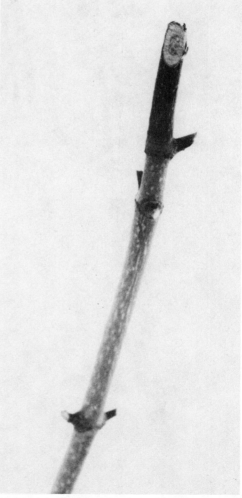

Twig that was snipped off neatly by feeding rabbit or hare. Note the angular cut.

Bark of this young aspen tree has been gnawed away by a rabbit or hare.

shows through on trees where bark has been gnawed off by the animals. Fallen branches and trees are especially attractive, and it's not unusual for all the bark within reach to be stripped in short order.

In fall and winter, rabbits and hares spend most of their time during the day under cover, often in one spot where they feel concealed and comfortable. Oval-shaped depressions develop in favored resting areas and these are called forms. Rabbits may go in holes in the ground or seek other shelter during cold weather, but they spend a lot of time above ground when the weather is moderate enough. I'm constantly amazed at how little cover it takes to conceal a cottontail. Countless times I've seen them streak away from depressions under clumps of grass to avoid being stepped on.

Hares are more tolerant of the cold than rabbits and spend most of their time in forms above ground, but they do occasionally tunnel down into the snow. One December I encountered a snowshoe hare using the same form day after day for at least a month. If it was chased away, it eventually returned. The form was underneath the fallen top of a white cedar tree. The shelter was open on one side, which made the hare easy to see, but he was covered from above, which was most important to protect him from hawks and owls. He was able to detect ground-based predators by sight or sound. The foliage on the cedar top was eventually eaten by deer, reducing its effectiveness in hiding the hare. At that point, the snowshoe moved to another, thicker blowdown nearby, and I suspect he spent the remainder of the winter there.

Hares that live in open country, such as Arctics and Europeans, huddle up next to what little cover is present. Both types of hares use forms next to rocks where they are protected from the wind but still have good visibility. White-tailed jacks hide in clumps of sagebrush, and blacktails take advantage of what cover they can find.

By learning to identify forms and noting their locations, it's possible for hunters to develop a feel for where their quarry is likely to hide and to seek out these spots. With experience, it also be-

comes possible to anticipate the appearance of a rabbit or hare and a possible shot, before it jumps into sight and starts to run. The same can be said for developing familiarity with and reading rabbit runways and hare trails, their feeding grounds, and their tracks.

For more information on wildlife sign of all types refer to my book *Animal Tracks and Signs of North America*.

Dark depression in foreground is form hare was occupying. Note the presence of droppings in the area.

Form of a European hare in New York next to rock. (Photo by Joe Dell)

4

Understanding Cycles

From the fall of 1972 through spring of 1974, South Fox Island, a chunk of Michigan real estate in Lake Michigan, was a snowshoe hare hunters' paradise. The prolific hares reached a population peak and maintained high levels for two and a half years.

I hunted deer on the island during November 1972 and recognized the potential for hare hunting. It was March 1973 before Jim Haveman and I returned to take advantage of the opportunity. By that time, all the islands of the Beaver Island chain were experiencing the same explosion of varying hares, and hunting regulations had been liberalized there. The bag limit and closed seasons were eliminated to serve as incentives for hunters. A short airplane ride or a long boat trip is required to reach the otherwise isolated islands.

Hares were everywhere on South Fox when Jim and I arrived. They were so abundant we decided to do our hunting with .22 handguns and bows. It was impossible to keep track of the misses, but by the end of a day of hunting we had 18 snowshoes between us. I didn't do much hunting, since I spent most of my time with cameras in my hands. Jim accounted for 14 of the total. If both of us had hunted hard, our tally would have easily reached 30 or more.

We weren't the only ones taking advantage of the abundant hares. There were snowy owls, rough-legged hawks, and goshawks on the island, and we occasionally encountered carcasses of snowshoes they fed on. There were certainly plenty of hares to go around.

While deer hunting on the island again in November 1973, a group of us took a few hours to gun-hunt hares and came up with about 30. Another afternoon I bowhunted on my own for a couple of

Jim Haveman and I bagged 18 snowshoe hares with bows and handguns during population peak.

hours, bagging 5 and missing many others. A caretaker at the hunting camp where we stayed said that about 400 snowshoes had been shot so far that year in the vicinity of the camp and about 1,000 on the island. He said he could count up to 34 jacks at a time from the porch of the camp any day during the summer.

I returned to South Fox for another hare hunt in March 1974 with Keith Chappel from Kingsley, who manages the hunting camp there. Snowshoes were still abundant, but not as much as the year before, and it looked like the population would decline further. There was severe damage to the island's vegetation from hungry hares. Saplings were girdled and many juniper bushes, which had been thick and green and had hidden numerous hares the previous year, were now dead. The remainder obviously couldn't hold up against the onslaught of snowshoes during the winter.

Four of us hunted together one day, primarily with rimfire .22s, and managed to collect 26 snow jacks between us, which is still good hunting. While afield we found one hare dead in a hole with no visible injuries, a sure sign of malnutrition.

There was a drop in the South Fox snowshoe hare population during 1974, but it was not a total crash. Fair numbers of hares remained for the next couple of years, although the vigor of the animals wasn't as high as it had been.

Jim Haveman and I visited the island again during November 1976, primarily for deer, and found enough hares to claim three with bows without much effort during a brief hunt for them. However, one of those three was not in the best of health. It was obviously small in size and lacked hair on its ears because of an infestation of tiny ticks.

I haven't been back since, but Keith Chappel told me snowshoes were relatively abundant again on the island from 1977 into 1980. By the spring of 1980, "They all had ticks in their ears and were running sideways," Keith said. The population nosedived and has been low for several years, but the animals are sure to rebound.

Snowshoe hare populations are cyclic, meaning they go through regular periods of highs and lows. The fluctuations in population numbers are extreme in some cases. A span of ten years between highs

Jim Haveman examines saplings girdled by hungry hares on South Fox Island, Michigan. Hare populations often crash during hard winters when they increase beyond their available food supply.

most of it may have been eliminated through overbrowsing by both animals by now. The presence of ground hemlock is sure to have played an important role in the cycle of hares on the island.

In locations where there is a good mix of habitat in various stages of succession or broken blocks of habitat, cycles are often moderated. In fact, hare populations may seem fairly constant without noticeable increases and decreases. Large expanses of similar habitat are most susceptible to typical hare cycles.

Snowshoe cycles are most pronounced in the northern part of their range, too, where long winters and short summers are common. Under these circumstances, the interaction between hares and their food supply becomes more critical than it is to the south. There is less food available during the winter because some of it is cov-

and lows is common, although the actual interval between cycles can be anywhere from eight to twelve years. On the Michigan mainland, records of snowshoe harvests, which correspond to population levels, indicate a ten-year cycle is in effect there. High harvests occurred during 1939–40, 1949–50, and 1959–60 and lows during 1944–45 and 1954–55. Harvest figures for the past twenty years indicate the timing of the cycle has changed somewhat, but 1984–85 was another low point.

The hare cycle on South Fox Island obviously doesn't correspond with the state as a whole, but I'm sure there are other areas in the state where this is true, too. The type and diversity of habitat can make a difference. When I was there, South Fox was unique in one respect: ground hemlock, a preferred food for both hares and deer, was abundant, but

Hunter dresses one of many snowshoe hares bagged on South Fox Island.

ered with snow, and that's when the jacks' need for a nutritious diet is the greatest to help them withstand the cold. Another factor that plays a role in the availability of food during this critical period will be discussed later.

Nova Scotia is on the southern edge of the snowshoe's range; a report from that province listed cyclic fluctuations in numbers there as moderate.

Although there can be variation in the timing of snowshoe hare cycles throughout their range, it is amazing how closely the most recent cycles correspond over a wide geographic area. An intensively studied population of hares near Rochester, Alberta, reached peaks during 1961, 1970, and 1980. Low populations were in 1965, 1975, and 1985. Highs were also reached at a couple of locations in the Yukon during 1980 and lows during 1985. The lows in Michigan certainly correspond with those in the two Canadian provinces.

Snowshoe hare populations are not the only ones that are cyclic. Fluctuations in numbers are also common for black-tailed and white-tailed jacks, Arctic, and tundra hares. European hares probably go through the same phases, too. Rabbit populations increase and decrease over periods of time, but not necessarily with the regularity and intensity that hares sometimes do. Nonetheless, cottontail populations can be considered cyclic, too, as far as the hunter is concerned, at least in some areas.

Interestingly enough, the most recent cycle of white-tailed and black-tailed jacks corresponds closely with the trend in snowshoe hare numbers. In Idaho, for example, blacktails peaked during 1980–81, and the harvest of whitetails in Minnesota reached a high point during 1980, going down steadily every year since. The harvest of snowshoe hares in Minne-

sota, incidentally, followed the same trend as for whitetails, hitting a high in 1980 and declining through 1984–85. Populations of black-tailed and white-tailed jacks were also at a low point in Kansas and Wyoming during 1985, to name a couple of examples I'm familiar with.

In Utah, blacktail cycles have ranged between seven and ten years. High harvests of whitetails in Iowa have occurred at four- to five-year intervals, but the overall trend has been downward. Total estimated harvest during the 1965–66 season was 133,000, 98,000 during 1969–70, 36,900 in 1974–75, and 26,000 during 1978–79. Each of the seasons listed was preceded by three or four years of declining harvests, with obvious increases at peaks.

Both long- and short-term population cycles have been identified for Arctic hares, with short-term cycles spanning three to five years and long-term about ten years in duration.

With cottontails, there is no consistent pattern of highs and lows from one state to the next. In southwestern Wyoming, severe winters are credited for reducing rabbits. Sightings of cottontails along census routes there dipped to almost zero per mile during 1970 after a peak in the mid-1960s. Populations rebounded slowly for a few years, then shot up to a high of more than six rabbits per mile of road in 1978. The winter of 1978–79 was another bad one, pushing cottontail sightings down to almost zero again by 1980.

Cottontail harvests in Missouri have decreased then increased again a couple of times over a sixteen-year period, but there have never been any real dramatic changes. The shifts have been gradual. The highest harvest from 1967 through 1982 was in 1967, when an estimated 2,673,377 were bagged. The kill remained over the two million mark for five more years, then dipped below two million for two years, reaching a low of 1,693,334 during 1974. Harvest figures were back over two million again in 1975 and 1976, before dropping below that magic figure for the next four years. The all-time low harvest for the sixteen-year period came in the third year (1979), 1,283,942. By 1981 the kill was back over two million and reached 2,300,117 in 1982.

Based on harvest estimates, Missouri's cottontail population is obviously fairly consistently high with minor, short-term fluctuations. More noticeable variations in harvests are apparent for Minnesota, however, a state in the snowbelt like Wyoming. Over a five-year period from 1979 through 1983 the kill went from 188,000 cottontails to 263,000 in 1981 and back down to 98,000 in 1983.

The best theory I can come up with in regard to cottontail populations, based on limited information, is that those in the northern part of their range, where winters are periodically hard, are subject to more pronounced changes than those in the south. This makes sense in view of what researchers have documented with snowshoe hares. So northern cottontails can be considered cyclic, but on a more irregular basis than hares. There was a ten-year span, however, between low points in the southwestern Wyoming rabbit population (1970 and 1980). It will be interesting to see if that trend continues.

Most of the research on hare and rabbit population cycles has been done on snowshoe hares because periodic changes in their numbers are predictable and sometimes dramatic. What has been learned about the causes of these cycles may very well apply to other hares, and rabbits, too. For many years, biologists and ecologists have been trying to fit the pieces of the snowshoe cycle puzzle together to better

understand why it occurs with such regularity. Some questions remain, but researchers are now closer than ever to solving the mystery.

Crashes of snowshoe populations are basically initiated in favorable habitat. In these good conditions they increase to a point where there isn't enough food to sustain them during the winter, and many of them die. Some starve and others are taken by predators. The weakened condition of many hares, especially juveniles, during such a winter, makes them more susceptible to predators, including man. Snow jacks that survive the winter are stressed further during the spring when breeding begins, which accounts for more losses. I think this is what caused the death of the snowshoe Keith Chappel and I found in a hole during March 1974 on South Fox Island.

Productivity of young hares is usually poor from females that survive through spring the year of a population slump, due to their poor health. After a major decline, snowshoe populations may decrease further for another two or three years. Biologists have only recently been able to explain why. It's the result of an interaction with the remaining hares and their food supply during the winter.

After being heavily browsed the previous winter, the trees, as a defense mechanism to protect new growth, produce resins that are toxic to snowshoes. Research has shown that jacks can detect these toxic chemicals and avoid them, even though the trees are their preferred food species. It's usually the third winter after a crash before a significant supply of food is available to snowshoes again.

From that point on, winter survival rates improve, along with productivity, and the population of hares starts rebuilding again. As long as winter food supplies

Predators like this Canada lynx do not control snowshoe hare populations. On the contrary, hares are responsible for the numbers of predators present. Lynx cycles in Canada follow those of the snowshoe hare by two or three years.

improve, conditions are favorable for the number of snowshoes to increase. Weather, disease, and predation all play roles in the rise and fall of snowshoe hare populations, but the most important factor is their relationship with their food supply.

Weather simply intensifies or eases the crisis when an overpopulation exists. Diseases and parasites are side effects or symptoms of a population out of balance with its food supply.

Population declines occur even in the absence of predators. Hawks, owls, lynx, bobcats, coyotes, and foxes take advantage of a high hare population that begins to go downhill in the same way that hunters do. They don't cause the slump. In fact, hares are more responsible for the abundance of predators than predators are responsible for the number of snowshoes present. A close correlation between snowshoe hare cycles and the number of lynx in Canada has been documented. Lynx cycles usually follow those of the hares, which are their primary prey, by two or three years.

Although 1984–85 was the low point in the population cycle of many hares and some rabbits, hunters should take heart knowing numbers will generally be on the increase from here on out. High levels can be expected by the late 1980s, with a peak around 1990 or before. Population peaks of rabbits and hares are the hunters' delight and lows can be frustrating, but that's the nature of the beasts. It's difficult to have one without the other.

Dedicated rabbit and hare hunters have to learn to take the good with the bad. Even during years when low populations are present, hunters who are serious about collecting some of these popular game animals, and know what they're doing, can still find action.

As an example, last winter was one of the poorest I've seen for snowshoe hares in upper Michigan for many years. There just weren't many of them around. It was difficult to find a track in some of our normal hunting grounds. So we scouted for new spots and found bunnies. One pleasant afternoon, Uncle George, his son Craig, and I collected three snowshoes. It wasn't a record bag by any means, but we had a good time and had something to show for our efforts at the end of the day. What more can a hunter ask for?

5

The Truth About Tularemia

The chances of hunters contracting tularemia from rabbits or hares are probably not as high as many of them think. The risks vary depending on where you do your hunting. In some states, the odds of coming in contact with tularemia are practically nonexistent, while in others hunters should take precautions.

As an example of a hunter's chances of handling a tularemic rabbit, consider the experience of Ken Sadler, supervisor of wildlife research for the Missouri Department of Conservation. In over 20 years he autopsied more than 12,000 cottontails, far more than an average hunter would handle in a lifetime. Many of them were found dead and were examined for cause of death—only two of those rabbits had tularemia. And Missouri had the second highest number of cases of tularemia reported in the United States during 1983

and 1984. So even in states where the incidence of the disease is among the highest in the country, the chances of coming in contact with it are slim.

Only 292 cases of tularemia were reported in the United States during 1984, according to the U.S. Department of Health and Human Services. During 1983, 310 individuals were treated for tularemia. No figures are available on how the affected individuals became sick, but rabbits are probably responsible for transmission of tularemia in only a fraction of the cases.

Rabbits and hares are only two of a number of possible carriers of the disease. Tularemia has been identified in 80 species of mammals, including muskrats, beavers, squirrels, and woodchucks. Some of these mammals have been responsible for passing on tularemia to hunters and trappers. Biting insects such as ticks, flies, lice, and fleas are generally responsible for more cases of tularemia than rabbits. People can get the disease from infected water, too.

Of the known causes of tularemia in Missouri over a 30-year period (1949–1979), tick bites accounted for 26 percent of them and contact with rabbits only 13 percent. Other mammals were responsible for 3 percent of the cases. The cause of approximately 57 percent of the cases was unknown. Contact with rabbits can probably be ruled out in most, if not all, of the unknown cases because rabbits are well-known carriers of tularemia and would have been identified as the cause if infected persons had any recent contact with the animals. In New York, only one-third of 44 cases of tularemia were attributed to wild rabbits.

The above information from Missouri and New York is an indication that rabbits are less responsible for transmitting tularemia to hunters than they used to be. By comparison, public health records for Illinois during the period 1926–1951 show that all cases of the disease were traceable to contact with cottontails. Cottontails, by the way, become infected with tularemia far more often than hares. Jack rabbits have been responsible for the transmission of tularemia to some people, but very few hunters have contracted the disease from snowshoe hares.

There has been a dramatic decline of tularemia among residents of the United States since 1955. That year there were approximately 0.35 cases reported per 100,000 people. In 1975 the rate of occurrence had dropped to an all-time low of 0.06 cases per 100,000 (129 cases). The disease has increased in frequency since then to between 0.12 and 0.16 per 100,000 during recent years; however, it still occurs far

less often than during the 1950s and so should not be of major concern to hunters.

During 1983, 90 percent of the reported cases of tularemia came from 20 states (see Table 1). Interestingly enough, those same states also accounted for 90 percent of the cases recorded during 1984. The risk of coming in contact with tularemia is obviously highest in those states, but it can be minimized if proper precautions are taken. Another 18 states were credited with less than five cases of the disease during 1983 and 1984 (see Table 2), and in some states (see Table 3) there were *no* instances of the sickness reported for those two years. However, keep in mind that Vermont is the only state where no cases of tularemia have *ever* been reported. The disease has been reported in Canadian provinces, too.

Table 1

States with At Least 5 Cases of Tularemia During 1983 and 1984

State	1983 Cases	1984 Cases
Arkansas	65	84
California	3	8
Colorado	19	8
Idaho	2	8
Illinois	2	8
Kansas	11	3
Louisiana	6	7
Massachusetts	3	7
Mississippi	5	1
Missouri	51	45
Montana	8	3
Nebraska	8	–
Nevada	1	5
North Carolina	8	1
Oklahoma	34	23
South Dakota	10	34
Tennessee	17	5
Texas	13	8
Wyoming	7	1
Utah	9	4

Table 2

States with Less Than 5 Cases of Talaremia in 1983 and 1984

State	1983 Cases	1984 Cases
Alaska	1	–
Arizona	1	4
Georgia	1	4
Kentucky	1	1
Maryland	4	2
Michigan	1	1
Minnesota	1	1
New Mexico	4	3
New Jersey	–	1
New York	1	2
North Dakota	1	–
Ohio	–	2
Oregon	3	2
Pennsylvania	3	–
Rhode Island	1	–
Virginia	1	1
Washington	2	4
Wisconsin	2	–

Table 3

States with No Reported Cases of Tularemia in 1983 and 1984

Alabama
Connecticut
Delaware
Florida
Indiana
Iowa
Maine
New Hampshire
South Carolina
Vermont
West Virginia

Oklahoma hunter Thayne Smith and his stepson Jeff accounted for two of the tularemia cases in that state. Jeff lives in Kansas but hunted with his stepfather in Oklahoma on New Year's Day that year. They were actually after quail but bagged two or three cottontails while afield. At the end of the day, Jeff skinned and cleaned the rabbits, then handed them to Thayne, who rinsed them with water and cut them in pieces. The rabbit meat was then cooked in a smoker and eaten. Within 24 hours, Jeff became ill, and his condition worsened over the next few days. Both Jeff and his doctor thought he had influenza and that's what he was treated for, with no results.

Three days after contact with the infected rabbit Thayne became sick. He had a high fever and ached all over. Two days later, he saw his doctor, who accurately diagnosed his ailment as tularemia. Thayne scratched a hand on briars while hunting and one of those scratches had become infected. That tipped the doctor off. Thayne also had swollen lymph nodes under his arms, another tularemia symptom. A blood test confirmed the diagnosis.

Jeff's doctor was then contacted and appropriate treatment was begun. By that time, Jeff had chest pains and his doctor thought he had developed pneumonia. Due to the advanced stage of the disease, it took Jeff a week to recover in the hospital. Thayne was cured in four days by taking antibiotics (tetracycline) at home.

Thayne could only guess, but he thought Jeff became sick first because he got a larger dose of bacteria while cleaning the infected rabbit. Jeff had injured a thumb and the wound wasn't healed when he handled the rabbits. The broken skin on his thumb was the source of his infection.

Thayne described his own bout with tularemia as the worst case of flu he ever had, with tremendous aches and pains and a high fever. The only reason Jeff became sicker, of course, is because his illness was not diagnosed and treated during its early stages.

Rabbits and hares that have tularemia act sick, at least during the advanced stages (they usually die within seven days). They simply don't behave normally; they appear tame or have difficulty running. However, the cottontails Thayne and Jeff bagged on that New Year's Day acted normally and appeared healthy. So they had no reason to suspect any of the bunnies were infected with tularemia.

How could they have protected themselves from the disease? The best way would have been to wear rubber gloves while handling the rabbits. This is a recommended practice whenever cleaning rabbits when the skin on your hand has been broken by a scratch or cut. Thin surgical gloves can be purchased cheaply from many drugstores. Rabbit hunters living in states with the highest number of tularemia cases reported, such as Arkansas, Missouri, Oklahoma, and South Dakota, would be wise always to wear gloves when cleaning rabbits, just to be on the safe side.

Thorough cooking of meat from an infected rabbit will kill the tularemia bacteria. However, it is generally best to dispose of the carcass of a rabbit that has this disease. Local health departments or personnel in labs at state wildlife agencies may be interested in examining the carcass of a rabbit that has tularemia, so try reporting it before discarding the carcass.

Examination of the liver is the best way to determine if any animal has tularemia. The liver, which is a dark red, flat organ found in the abdominal cavity near the diaphragm, will be covered with numerous small white spots if the animal is infected. Refer to the accompanying photo as an example of what to look for.

If you are handling with bare hands a rabbit that proves to have a spotted liver,

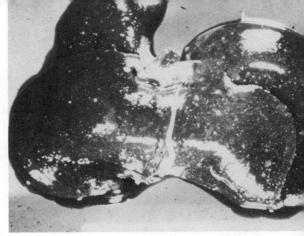

Liver from animal with tularemia. Note large number of small, white spots. (Photo by Michigan Department of Natural Resources)

clean hands thoroughly with soap and hot water after disposing of the carcass. Contact a physician if a fever or other symptoms of illness develop.

Rabbits encountered in the field that act sick should be shot, if possible, then buried or covered with rocks, wood, or vegetation. Try to avoid touching the carcass during this process. Cottontails that are easily caught by a dog should be treated in the same fashion.

Hares and rabbits may carry at least one other disease besides tularemia, plus parasites, none of which pose a threat to man. Hunters' failure to differentiate between tularemia and these other afflictions has led to the needless waste of rabbits and hares in the past. To help prevent this in the future, the most common diseases and parasites hunters might see in or on rabbits and hares will be discussed next.

Sometimes you may bag cottontails and hares that have wartlike growths somewhere on their bodies, usually on feet, legs, ears, head, or back. These warts may be small and rounded or several inches long and pointed like spikes, but they can take on any shape. They are called *fibromas* and are caused by a virus transmitted to the animals by biting insects, most often mosquitoes.

Although fibromas may appear unsightly in severe cases, they are only on the skin and do not affect the edibility of meat. The warts or tumors are removed with the skin. The virus that causes fibromas in rabbits is not transmissible to humans by touching the infected areas or handling the rabbit.

My only experience with fibromas was on a recent hunt with Wayne Van Zwoll for cottontails in Kansas. Two of the bunnies bagged had fibromas and one of them had a number of the growths around its mouth. The second cottontail had a large, odd-shaped growth on the top of its head between the ears; at first I thought it was a large seed pod of some type that got caught in its hair.

A photo of one of these animals is included in this chapter. Fibromas on rabbits have been reported in a number of states and may be more common during some years than others.

Parasites are responsible for other growths and infections found in or on rab-

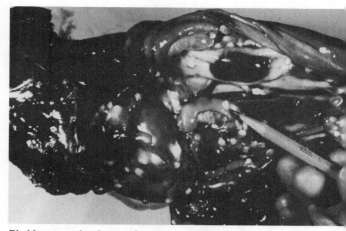

Bladderworms in viscera of a cottontail. These are tapeworm cysts that can infect dogs if ingested. (Photo by Michigan Department of Natural Resources)

bits and hares. *Bladderworms*, which are a larval stage of tapeworms common in cottontails and snowshoe hares, cause the most concern among hunters because they occur most often in the body cavity and may cause discoloration of the liver like tularemia. These parasites are harmless to humans, however, and are removed during the dressing process.

Bladderworms are small (⅛–¼ inch in diameter) fluid-filled, jellylike sacs or cysts about the size of grains of rice. White spots inside the otherwise clear sacs are the larval tapeworms. Bladderworms may be numerous throughout the body cavity, sometimes concentrated in the anal area or clinging to internal organs such as the liver, intestines, and stomach. They may be present singly or in clumps.

Before migrating into the body cavity, bladderworms spend some time in their hosts' liver and may leave whitish streaks or bands of scar tissue. This is different from the many tiny white spots that dot the livers of rabbits infected with tularemia. Hunters should try not to confuse

Cottontail with fibromas, which are wartlike and do not affect meat of animals that have them.

liver scarring caused by bladderworms and the spotting of tularemia.

The cysts of another type of tapeworm that is common to snowshoe hares, but may also occur in cottontails, are found in fluid-filled swellings or blisters under the skin or between muscles. These blisters contain a number of cysts similar to bladderworms, but they are larger and more elongated. In addition, each fluid-filled sac contains a number of white spots or larval tapeworms rather than just one.

I've most often found these larval tapeworm blisters on the hind legs of snowshoe hares. The cysts and fluid are easily drained from blisters, leaving edible meat. Even if the cysts aren't removed, they would be killed during cooking.

Rabbits and hares are intermediate hosts for these types of tapeworms. They develop into the adult form only when ingested by members of the dog or cat family such as foxes, coyotes, or bobcats, which routinely prey on bunnies. Rabbit hunting dogs can also become infected with these parasites if they ingest the cysts, so hunters should be sure to discard entrails from rabbits and hares in a manner that they won't be accessible to their pets. Hunters who feed their dogs meat from rabbits or hares they bag should boil the meat first to kill any larval tapeworms that might be present.

Larval *bot flies*, called grubs, bots, or warbles, are sometimes found on or just under the skin of rabbits in the neck region and around legs (see photo). Like larval tapeworms, they pose no danger to humans. These parasites are usually removed during the skinning process. In some cases it may be desirable to trim the area under the skin where grubs were attached. Larval bot flies drop off of rabbit hosts during early fall, so they are most often en-

Two bot fly larvae are visible under the skin of neck of this cottontail. One on right is dark in color and more developed than white one on left. (Photo by Michigan Department of Natural Resources)

countered early in the season. In some states these parasites have left hosts by the time hunting season opens.

One other parasite that hunters may notice in rabbits or hares occurs in muscles as whitish, threadlike streaks. These streaks are parallel to muscle fibers and are noticed most often when sectioning meat. They are a larval stage of *sarcocystis parasites* and are killed during cooking, so hunters need not worry about their presence.

With the exception of tularemia, there is no disease or larval parasite carried by rabbits and hares that hunters should be concerned about. The chances of coming in contact with tularemia appear to be much lower than formerly thought, and hunters in states and provinces where tularemia is most common can reduce the odds on contracting it even further by taking the precautions mentioned in this chapter. Knowing how to identify tularemia properly, as well as other diseases and parasites common to rabbits and hares, will help keep hunters healthy and prevent the needless waste of good meat.

6

Guns and Loads

A near-perfect gun for all-around rabbit and hare hunting is an over-and-under combination that is both a rifle and shotgun, with the rifle barrel designed for shooting .22 caliber rimfire ammunition and a 20-gauge shotgun with the barrel bored improved cylinder.

The .22 would be the choice for sitting shots at bunnies where there is an opening large enough to sneak one of the small bullets through. The shotgun would come into play on shots at moving targets or in brush thick enough to deflect a .22 bullet. On shots at sitting rabbits that miss their mark, the shotgun barrel would provide a perfect followup shot. However, the .22 round would be a poor second chance at a running rabbit or hare.

An inherent problem with rifle/shotgun combinations is that they are invariably single-shot models, holding one rifle and shotgun cartridge each. One shot from either or both barrels is sometimes not enough to make good on an opportunity at a rabbit or hare. However, I don't think there is any firearm that is a perfect choice for all rabbit and hare hunting circumstances.

The truth is, there isn't a combination gun of the type mentioned in the first paragraph that is presently manufactured. Savage makes the only .22 rimfire/shotgun combo. The shotgun gauges these over-and-unders come in are .410 and 20, and all shotguns come with full choke barrels. However, the chokes of shotgun barrels can be changed. Savage's service department will add screw-in chokes to change full-choke 20s to improved cylinder or any other choke desired. Contact

Andy Tingstad with snowshoe hare bagged with .22 rifle/shotgun combination, a near-perfect gun for rabbit and hare hunting.

Savage service headquarters at 330 Lockhouse Rd., Westfield, MA 01085 (413/562-4196).

Besides the .22 rimfire and shotgun combinations, Savage has other rifle calibers over shotguns. They are the .22 magnum, .22 hornet, .222, .223 and .30-30. Rifle barrels are also bored for two calibers normally reserved for handguns, the .357 magnum and .357 maximum. Only 20-gauge shotgun barrels are combined with rifle barrels in centerfire calibers.

Velmet, Inc. (7 Westchester Plaza, Elmsford, NY 10523 (914/347-4440) makes rifle/shotgun combinations, too, but not with the .22 rimfire. Their smallest calibers are .222 and .223. These are on top of 12-gauge shotgun barrels with improved modified chokes, which apparently are a compromise between improved cylinder and modified.

Despite the fact that combination guns can be nearly perfect for collecting rabbits and hares under a variety of situations, most of these small game animals are shot either with a rifle or shotgun. From the point of practicality, most hunters use a dual-purpose gun, one that is chosen first and foremost for upland birds or waterfowl in the case of scatterguns, and for squirrels in the case of .22 rifles. These same guns are also used to bag rabbits and hares.

Actually, a variety of guns and loads are suitable as well as adequate for these popular game animals. Frankly, I can't think of any shotgun that couldn't be used successfully to hunt rabbits, and that includes front-loading replicas in addition to modern scatterguns. Any type of .22 rimfire rifle, including air rifles that shoot pellets, and handguns also qualify as rabbit guns. Although the .22 rimfire is the most common rifle and handgun caliber used on hunts for hares and rabbits, certain centerfire and bigger bore blackpowder rifles and handguns can and have been used in this type of hunting, too.

The fact that the choice of guns for rabbits and hares is so wide is one reason hunting them is so popular. No hunters are excluded from the pursuit of these critters because they don't have a suitable gun. Hunters who are after squirrels, grouse, quail, woodcock, pheasant, ducks, geese, and more can also be classified as rabbit hunters, and in many cases they are. A lot of rabbits and hares are bagged as bonuses by hunters who are actually primarily after something else.

As mentioned earlier, I would rate a 20-gauge shotgun with the barrel bored improved cylinder as one of the best choices for hunting rabbits and hares. In the case of double-barreled models, the second barrel could have the same choke, but the gun's versatility would be increased if it were bored-cylinder or modified. The 20-gauge is usually light and fast handling and offers medium-weight loads, heavier than those available in the .410 and lighter than those for the 12 gauge. This makes it just right for cottontails and snowshoe hares, which are the species most hunted with shotguns. Twenty-gauge guns designed to handle 3-inch shells offer hunters the option of hunting with shells that are equivalent to light 12-gauge loads.

Standard 2¾-inch, 20-gauge shells from Federal come in three versions: 2½ drams equivalent of powder and 1 ounce of shot, 2¾ drams and 1 or 1⅛ ounces, or 3¼ drams and ¾ ounce of shot. Their 3-inch shells hold 3¼ drams of powder and 1 ounce of shot or 3 drams and 1¼ ounces. Any of these loads is suitable for hunting rabbits and hares.

Both snowshoe hares and the various varieties of cottontails are relatively easy to kill. They are thin-skinned, and it doesn't take many pellets to bring them down. However, there are sometimes not enough pellets in .410 shells to make clean kills consistently, especially in brushy habitat where much of the pattern is stopped short. The number of BBs in .410 shells also tends to limit the effective range of the smallest shotgun.

In regard to the 12-gauge, there are sometimes too many pellets. A rabbit or hare caught solidly in the pattern from a 12-gauge, especially at close range, is often riddled with shot, causing more damage than necessary. However, I have to admit that many of the rabbits and hares I've bagged over the years have fallen to a 12-gauge, and I don't recall any that weren't salvageable for the table, but there was meat loss in some cases.

Craig Smith hefts hare bagged with shotgun. These guns account for the majority of rabbits and hares bagged every year.

When you're after cottontails and varying hares, I would recommend use of the heaviest loads possible with a .410 (½ ounce of shot in 2½-inch shells and ¹¹/₁₆ ounce in 3-inch), and light to medium loads for the 12-gauge. Light 12-gauge loads would include 3 drams equivalent of powder and 1 or 1⅛ ounces of shot. Medium loads would hold 3¼ drams of powder and 1⅛ or 1¼ ounces of shot.

There are two other shotgun gauges that used to be made, and some of them are still in circulation—the 28 and 16. Twenty-eight-gauge shells come with ¾ ounce of lead from the factory, but hunters into handloading can develop loads containing ⅞ and 1 ounce of shot. Factory loads for the 16-gauge contain 2¾ drams of powder and 1⅛ ounces of shot.

Open-choked shotgun barrels such as improved-cylinder and cylinder are best for collecting rabbits and snowshoes because they throw the largest patterns, increasing the chances of connecting on racing bunnies. Open chokes also reduce the likelihood of overkill with 12-gauge guns at about 20 yards and beyond. These chokes perform their best at distances that the vast majority of shots for rabbits and snowshoes are taken.

Although the 20-gauge will still produce results for hunters who are after jacks, European hares, and Arctic hares, the 12-gauge with modified- or full-choke barrels would be better choices. These critters are not only larger than most snowshoe hares and cottontails, they usually occupy more open habitat than their relatives. As a result, shots at them average farther away and their size makes them harder to bring down.

Open-choked 12-gauges can be suitable for bagging these hares, though. Jack Burt from Wiarton, Ontario, still uses an old reliable, hunt-worn, pump 12-gauge on European hares; it probably has a cylinder bore now, and it does the job for him. The scattergun used to have a full-choke barrel until one day when he took a shot at a hare from an ice-covered road. Burt fell down at the shot, because of the icy footing, he thought. He did get the animal, though. It wasn't until later that he noticed the end of his shotgun barrel was ruptured and he realized his barrel had been plugged with snow when he shot the hare. Then he realized that he had been knocked down by extra recoil rather than slipping. Jack simply sawed off the barrel below the rupture and has used it as is ever since.

Shotgun actions are basically a matter of personal preference. Single shots, doubles, pumps and semiautomatics are available. If you're using a pump or semiauto

I'm holding up a hare bagged with double-barrel black-powder shotgun made by Navy Arms.

shotgun when there is a lot of snow on trees, try to keep as much snow as possible out of the action to prevent them from icing up and malfunctioning.

A pump shotgun has been my personal favorite for hunting hares and rabbits. I've needed and used more than two shots on a number of occasions. I plug my guns so they don't hold more than three shells, so I won't forget on a day I happen to go waterfowl hunting.

As far as shot sizes to use for rabbit and hare hunting, 6s and 7½s are both good choices for cottontails and snowshoes. Sixes can also be used for jacks, but 5s are better and 2s best. Twos are the top choice for European and Arctic hares, too.

The same discussion about the selection of modern shotguns and loads for rabbit hunting also applies to black-powder scatterguns. The major difference is that hunters have to bring all the components that are included in shotgun shells — shot, powder, wads, and primers — carrying them individually in pockets or a "possibles" bag, and put them together in the barrel or barrels for each shot.

I've used a double-barreled 12-gauge made by Navy Arms to collect rabbits and hares. The barrels have modified and full chokes because I originally obtained the gun for turkey hunting. The load I settled on is 3½ drams of powder and 1⅛ ounces of shot.

Most replica front-loading shotguns come with manuals that list the manufacturer's recommendations for loads. Experiment within the limits listed to determine which load performs best in your gun. Once a satisfactory load is determined, it is a good idea to mark your ramrod at the muzzle once a load is completed, to serve as future reference. The mark should always line up with the muzzle. If it doesn't, either one of the components is missing or too much of one of the items was added.

The .22 rimfire rifle with long rifle bullets is the best rifle for hunting rabbits and hares, period. I prefer solid bullets, but hollow points would be a better choice for jacks, European, and Arctic hares. Semiautomatic models are at the top of my list for performance, especially if there is a chance of running shots in the open. The action doesn't matter as much when plinking at sitting targets.

I use a .22 rifle over a shotgun for hunting rabbits and hares whenever possible. Bagging bunnies is often more challenging, and it's also more fun. However, shotguns are usually the better choice when hunting as part of a large group. When I do carry a .22 I go for head shots whenever possible, but don't hesitate to shoot for the chest when the head isn't visible. A hit in either location is deadly.

A few of the better .22 caliber air rifles are suitable for rabbit and hare hunting. I shot several snowshoe hares with Crosman's most powerful .22. Pellets for .22

The rimfire .22 rifle is also popular for rabbit and hare hunting.

Gene Brehm hefts a black-tailed jack bagged with a .32 caliber muzzle-loading rifle.

rifles for long-range hare hunting, but in fixed magnification scopes, he likes 6 power.

The closest caliber to the .22 in black-powder rifles is the .32. This is the best choice in muskets for hunting rabbits and hares, although larger calibers can also be used and might be fun to try out on jack rabbits. I've shot snowshoe hares with round balls from my .50-caliber Thompson/Center Hawken, going for head and chest shots.

Percussion-model replicas are better for this type of hunting than flintlocks, and the same is true for front-loading shot-

Tom Lowin from South Dakota used this semiautomatic .22 to bag white-tailed jack he's holding. Revolvers in the same caliber are good choices, too. (Photo by Ron Spomer)

air rifles come in two styles—pointed and flat. The pointed pellets are the choice for hunting.

Flat-shooting centerfire rifles are popular for hunting jack rabbits and are sometimes used on European and Arctic hares, too. Some of the best choices are the .22 magnum, .218, .22 hornet, .22 swift, .22/250, .222, and .223. However, any caliber centerfire rifle can be used on jacks as a means of preparing and practicing for big game hunting.

Bud Oakland from Coeur d'Alene, Idaho, has done a lot of jack rabbit hunting with the calibers mentioned above. He doesn't recommend the .22/250 or .22 swift in situations where a lot of shooting is involved. He said the barrels of these rifles heat up too fast. Oakland highly recommends variable scopes (3–9 power) on guns. As mentioned for black-powder shotguns, follow the manufacturer's recommendation when developing loads for muskets and experiment to determine which load performs best in your rifle.

Handguns chambered for .22 rimfire long rifles are super sporting choices for hunting rabbits and hares. I've taken my share of snowshoes with a revolver, but semiautomatics would be equally good bets.

Jacks would provide plenty of practice for centerfire handgun shooters using revolvers up to .44 magnums or the hot single-shot contenders made by Thompson/Center Arms in a variety of calibers. Here again, practice on jacks with centerfire handguns can be excellent preparation for big game hunting. The more the guns are used, the better hunters will be able to handle them.

Bud Oakland told me about a friend of his, Norman Young, who on one occasion made a remarkably long shot on a jack rabbit with a .44 magnum handgun with an 8½-inch barrel. There was a lot of luck involved, of course.

Oakland and Young were close to one another when the hare was jumped, and Bud did his best to bust it with his .22 swift. Norm waited as Bud took three shots, none of which connected. The running rabbit was over 200 yards away when Norm took a shot, holding his handgun one-handed. The bullet connected, folding the jack cleanly. Because the distance was so great, Bud stepped it off and came up with 255 yards. Bud said Norm insisted he simply waited for the right time to shoot and he wasn't at all surprised about the outcome. Young never fired the .44 again that day.

That just goes to show any gun can be used for hunting rabbits and hares. Whether you own a shotgun, rifle, a combination of the two, or a handgun, you are all set for hunting these most popular small game animals.

7

Bows and Arrows

It's been years since I shot my first rabbit with bow and arrow. I don't remember what year it was, but I do remember what type of equipment I was using. The bow was a low-priced model with solid fiberglass limbs and was rated at 45-pound pull. It had a plastic handle with rests on both sides for either right- or left-handed shooters. The arrow was made of cedar, was tipped with a field point, and had feather fletching.

There was a light covering of snow on the ground and I spotted the cottontail hunkered next to a brush pile. I was shooting instinctively at the time, having been told that's the way to go. Either my aim was good or it was that rabbit's unlucky day, but my arrow found its mark.

That cottontail was a real trophy for me then. As I recall, it was my first year of bowhunting and the first game I bagged

with bow and arrow. I remember many hunts before that one on which my arrows missed both cottontails and snowshoe hares. So making that kill was a momentous occasion. That's probably why the memory has stuck with me all these years.

The equipment I used to collect that cottontail was not the best-suited for rabbit or hare hunting, yet it served the purpose. As with shotguns, I don't think there are any bows and arrows that can't be used for this type of small game hunting. However, there is equipment that is better suited for it than others.

Just like guns, most bows and arrows used for rabbit and hare hunting were purchased primarily for hunting other game such as deer or perhaps for bowfishing. Hunters who use their archery equipment for both big and small game become more proficient with their gear. Small game hunting is actually super practice for big game hunting. It's possible to become familiar with archery tackle by shooting it under actual hunting conditions, when rabbits and hares are readily available. This is perfect preparation for the one or two shots an archer might get at deer, bear, or elk. Bowhunters who can consistently hit a target as small as a cottontail or snowshoe hare should be deadly on deer.

The minimum draw weight of the vast majority of hunting bows is between 35 and 40 pounds, which is more than adequate for taking rabbits and hares. However, bows as light as 20-pound pull should prove adequate for taking bunnies, providing the arrows released from them are tipped with broadheads, according to bowhunting veteran George Gardner from Detroit, Michigan. He said bows as light as 30-pound pull should do the job with blunt-tipped arrows.

A more detailed discussion of arrows and arrowheads will come later. There's more to be said about bows first. A number of different styles of bows are available today—the English long or straight bow, recurves, and compounds—all of them suitable for rabbit hunting.

Longbows are actually straight when unstrung and, as their name implies, are the longest bows made. They vary from 70 to 78 inches in length. When strung, these bows form a uniform uninterrupted curve from tip-to-tip. English longbows represent the earliest bow design.

John Shoals from Cody, Wyoming, does a lot of bowhunting for both big game and rabbits, all of it with a 70-pound-pull longbow. John's father manufactures longbows.

Recurve bows represent an improved design over longbows; they throw a faster arrow with shorter limbs (up to 190 feet

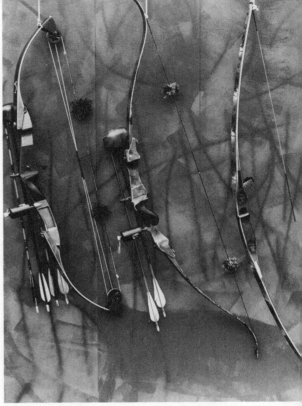

Three styles of bows available. From left to right they are a compound, recurve, and English longbow.

per second versus 170–185 for arrows from longbows). Limbs of recurves curve inward at sharper arcs than longbows, then bend outward near their tips. This style of bow varies from 50 to 68 inches in length. The longer recurves are smoother drawing and usually perform better than extremely short models. However, the shorter a bow is, the easier it is to maneuver in the heavy cover that some cottontails and snowshoe hares are found in. Bow length is of little consequence when hunting in open habitat.

Compounds represent the latest bow design, incorporating cables and pulleys or cams with a bow string and limbs to produce arrow speeds generally faster than those from comparable draw-weight recurves. Compound bows have other advantages, too, that make them so popular today. These bows make it possible to shoot heavy draw weights while holding only a fraction of that weight (30 to 50 percent) at full draw.

Longbows and recurves become progressively harder to pull and hold the farther they are drawn, with maximum strain on arms and fingers realized at full draw. This makes it difficult to hold heavy hunting bows of those styles at full draw for long without getting shaky and affecting accuracy. Compound bows, on the other hand, are hardest to draw when the arrow is only a fraction of the way back toward an archer's anchor point. When the string is pulled far enough that the pulleys or power cams "roll over," the holding weight "drops off" or relaxes a certain percentage, depending on the type of compound used. This feature allows hunters to hold an arrow at full draw longer to aim better than would be possible with a comparable weight recurve or long bow. A hunter using a 50-pound-pull compound with a 50 percent letoff in draw weight, for example, would be holding only 25 pounds at full draw.

One more advantage compounds have over recurves and English longbows is they are available in adjustable draw weights, with 10 to 15 pounds of pull difference between recommended minimum and maximum draw weights. A compound can be adjustable from 35- to 50-pound pull or 40 to 50, as well as many other variations. This has distinct advantages for young or beginning bowhunters who might want to start out at 35-pound pull for rabbit hunting and eventually work up to 45- or 50-pound pull for deer hunting. Once the heavier draw weight can be handled comfortably, the same weight can be used for rabbit hunting. In fact,

hunting rabbits and hares with bow and arrow is a perfect way for youngsters and novice hunters to prepare for deer hunting. It doesn't hurt the experienced archer's chances of success one bit either.

Because compounds have a more complicated design, it's easier for something to happen to them that would affect the way they shoot. Compounds must be properly tuned to achieve the best arrow flight. Bow tuning can be done by a qualified dealer or, with a good book on the subject, you can do it yourself.

While compounds remain strung at all times, with the possible exception of when a string is being replaced or the bow repaired, straight and recurve bows can and should be unstrung at the end of the day of hunting. Bow stringers should be used to string and to unstring recurve and longbows to prevent twisting the limbs.

Hunters must know their draw length before purchasing a compound bow to make sure they get one that fits them. Draw length also comes into play for purchasing arrows of the appropriate length. An easy way to determine draw length is to put one end of a yardstick at the center of your chest, parallel to the floor, and extend your arm and hand along it. The measurement at the tips of fingers is your draw length. Draw length can also be determined by drawing a premeasured and calibrated arrow shaft with a bow. The measurement that corresponds with where an arrow tip should be when at full draw is the desired length.

It is important to purchase arrows matched to a bow's draw weight. If you're unsure of the draw weight of a bow, have it tested on a scale. Determine both the peak and holding weights of compound bows. The draw weight of some bows changes over a period of time, so it is ad-

Dan White from Wyoming readies a blunt-tipped arrow on a recurve bow for shot at cottontail at far right in front of log under evergreen tree.

visable to have this checked periodically. Draw weights of recurve and longbows are based on a 28-inch draw length. Three pounds of draw weight can be added or subtracted for each inch of draw length more than or less than 28.

Arrow shafts are made from aluminum, fiberglass, fiberglass and graphite combined (graphlex), and wood (cedar). Wood shafts should not be used with compound bows but can be shot from recurve and longbows. Cedar arrows are more susceptible to warping than those made from other materials, but they're also cheaper, which is definitely a consideration for rabbit hunting where arrows may be routinely lost or broken.

John Shoals shoots cedar arrows out of his longbow when rabbit hunting because he said it's not unusual to break anywhere from 10 to 20 arrows a day when chasing cottontails. There are a lot of rocks in the areas he hunts, which accounts for the arrow damage.

Although I used to hunt rabbits and hares with wood shafts and a recurve bow, I now use aluminum arrows out of a compound. Several types of aluminum shafts are available with the price tag increasing along with their quality and durability. Easton's American Eagle aluminum shafts are the cheapest, for example, with Game Getters intermediate in price range and XX75s the most expensive.

As for arrowheads, blunts or broadheads are better for hunting rabbits and hares than field or target points. Whenever possible, I use blunts over broadheads when after bunnies because they produce more shocking power than cutting heads and don't damage the carcass as much. I prefer flat metal blunts to other types.

The simplest metal blunts are made from empty .38 or .357 revolver ammunition cases glued to the end of cedar shafts. I collected my first bow-bagged snowshoe hare with such an arrow. The hare was hunkered in the snow near a road in the woods that three of us were walking along. It remained motionless, probably hoping its natural camouflage would make it invisible, but the animal's brown eyes tipped me off to its presence.

I now use replaceable metal blunts on the end of aluminum arrows. The Game Tracker Company in Flushing, Michigan, manufactures a new plastic blunt, plus a rubber tip that pulls over the end of arrow shafts, converting them to blunts; I hope to try them on rabbits and hares in the future.

Whenever hunting rabbits and hares in the snow I use a string tracker such as the one made by Game Tracker to attach to my arrows. It makes the shafts easy to find after a missed shot. Otherwise, shafts become buried in snow and can be difficult, if not impossible, to relocate. A string tracker enables me to use good aluminum shafts without having to worry about losing them. I pick up all used string after each shot, of course. Hunters who aren't willing to pick up after themselves should not use these arrow-finding devices.

Fletching for arrows can be either plastic vanes or feathers. Choosing which to use is a matter of personal preference; however, feathers with a helical twist generally straighten more quickly and are more forgiving of a sloppy release than vanes. If vanes are used, those with a helical twist usually fly better than straight ones.

A *quiver* of some type will be necessary to carry arrows while rabbit hunting. I prefer the type that attaches directly to bows because they prevent arrows from rattling and keep them handy for followup shots. Rabbits or hares that are missed with an arrow will sometimes stay put long enough for a second or third shot.

Michigan bowhunter Gene Ballew holds up snowshoe hare he bagged with bow and arrow. Note Game Tracker (black cylinder) on front of his bow and bow quiver containing arrows. Large fletched arrows, called flu-flus, don't fly as far as normally fletched arrows would, making them good choices for small game hunting.

I remember one time emptying my quiver of four arrows when trying to bag a snowshoe hare sitting tight in a patch of hazel brush. After I was out of arrows I put my camera into action, capturing the hare's image on film before it finally vacated the premises.

Back and belt quivers are also available. Some back quivers hold more arrows than the belt or bow variety, making them advantageous when hunting areas loaded with rabbits and hares.

I highly recommend *bow sights* for beginning bowhunters who have trouble placing arrows consistently. Some archers

A back quiver is sometimes a better choice for hunting when rabbits and hares are abundant because it holds more arrows. A pair of snowshoe hares that are beginning to turn white are shown with recurve bow that was used to bag them.

have the natural ability to shoot arrows accurately without a sight, instinctively knowing where to hold the bow before releasing. Others use the tip of their arrow as a point of reference for aiming. Other archers, such as myself, need a specific aiming point or sight to place arrows accurately with consistency. Bow sights are simply brackets that fit in sight windows containing from one to four or five colored pins, which can be set for different distances, usually in 5- to 10-yard increments. I'm presently using two sight pins, one set for 10 yards and the other for 20.

When adjusting sight pins, the general rule is to "follow the arrow." If arrows are hitting left of center, move the pin to the left, which should shift the point of impact of subsequent arrows to the right. When arrows are hitting low of where you want them to, lower the sight pin.

Either a *finger tab*, leather shooting glove, or release aid should be used on your hand to hold and release the bow string. Tabs and gloves are best suited for most hunting conditions, although some hunters employ release aids. Release aids usually give more consistent releases than when using fingers on the string. Tabs often give smoother, more consistent, releases than gloves.

A *nocking point* is important so arrows are nocked (put on the string) in the same place for each shot. Arrows are normally nocked under nocking points. Nocking points should be added to bow strings $\frac{1}{8}$ inch to $\frac{1}{2}$ inch above a point perpendicular to the arrow rest or shelf. Feather-fletched arrows can be shot off of either a rest or shelf. Vanes can be shot only from an arrow rest. Nock sets, which are nothing more than small metal rings with a rubber lining, make great nocking points. They are clamped tightly in place with a pair of pliers.

Armguards are another accessory beginning bowhunters should consider using. These pieces of leather strap on the forearm of the arm that is holding the bow and keep loose clothing out of the way of the string when an arrow is released; they also protect the forearm from being slapped by the string if the bow isn't held properly.

For more specific information on archery and bowhunting, I suggest you refer to books devoted entirely to these subjects. It's also a good idea to join a local archery or bowhunting club to get first-hand advice from experienced archers.

8

Clothing and Accessories

The guidelines for what to wear on a rabbit or hare hunt are as stringent as those for selecting a gun or bow. It doesn't really matter much what you wear, as long as it's comfortable and keeps you warm and dry. Blue jeans and boots of various shapes, sizes, and styles, combined with a hodgepodge of shirts, sweaters, sweatshirts, and coats are standard apparel for bunny hunts.

What the weather is like at the time of a hunt actually has a lot to do with what types and how much clothing to wear; it also dictates the best choice of boots, hats, and gloves. Local regulations also come into play. Some fabrics and clothing colors are not only better for small game hunting than others, some are required. Many states and provinces now require that small game hunters wear a minimum amount of orange material, for example,

to reduce the chances of accidents, and you should of course follow these regulations.

In Michigan, gun hunters have a choice of wearing a hat, vest, or coat that is orange. Other states require at least an orange vest. Although orange garments are more readily visible to game than natural greens and browns, this alone shouldn't have much bearing on success when hunting rabbits and hares. It's more important that garments, whatever their color, be made of soft, quiet material that doesn't make noise as a hunter moves.

Goose down coats or vests with nylon shells, for instance, can help keep hunters warm during cold weather. However, the nylon is extremely noisy, drawing unnecessary attention to the hunter wearing it. The noise factor makes nylon a poor choice in outerwear for rabbit hunting. I remember a blue nylon-covered goose down coat that George wore on at least one hunt with dogs. A hare that was ahead of hounds, and that got by me, popped out in front of George. The noisy nylon coat gave away his position as he raised his gun, and the snowshoe streaked away before he could get a shot off.

The key to being comfortable when rabbit and hare hunting, regardless of prevailing weather conditions and the hunting technique used, is to dress in layers. Under the warmest of conditions, one layer of clothing—a light shirt and pair of pants or a one-piece jumpsuit—may suffice. As temperatures drop, layers are added, with individual garments becoming heavier so each layer provides as much insulation against the cold as possible.

By dressing in layers, rabbit and hare hunters can easily adjust their clothing throughout the day to remain comfortable as temperatures rise and fall or their activity level increases or decreases. Temperatures are frequently at their lowest point early in the morning and sometimes increase dramatically after a few hours of sunshine. Hunters dressed in layers can remove a layer or two if they become too warm. The same goes for the hunter who may have been sitting or moving slowly, then shifts into a faster pace. Even though the air temperature may not have changed, an increase in activity will heighten the feeling of warmth and a layer or two can be shed to return to the comfort level.

Small backpacks are well suited for storing extra layers of clothes, as well as some accessories that will be mentioned later. Moving hunters who lack a pack can tie sweaters or sweatshirts around their waists with the sleeves.

Smith's Law says, Dress for the coldest temperature expected during the day, or at least bring along enough layers for those conditions. Hunters can always remove layers if they get too warm, but they can't put on layers they don't have. Each individual has different temperature tolerances, and the amount of clothing it will take to keep hunters comfortable at various temperature ranges can best be determined by trial and error.

Decisions on how many layers to wear will also be dictated by the hunting technique used. I dress differently on days I will be sitting, for example, than for outings where I will be participating in drives or plan to follow tracks in the snow. More clothing is required to remain warm when at a stand than when on the move much of the time, of course.

The well-dressed hare hunter—wool outer shirt and pants, Jones-style hat in orange, and Sorel boots. Wool is soft, quiet, and warm, a good choice for winter hunts.

I always wear long-sleeve shirts when rabbit or hare hunting in thick cover, no matter how warm it gets, to protect my arms from scratches as well as biting insects. Short-sleeve shirts are a better choice for hunting relatively open habitat when it's warm, as long as biting insects aren't a problem.

Wool is the absolute best material for cold-weather hunting, in my opinion. It's warm and retains warmth when wet, it's soft and quiet, and it's available in popular colors for hunters—orange, red, and green. I wear wool pants, shirts, sweaters, and coats when hunting in cool to cold weather, not necessarily all at once. Plaid patterns are popular in wool shirts and coats. Sweaters are available in regular or winter camouflage patterns as well as in orange and black. Pants come in gray, greens, and reds.

Acrylic sweaters are as good as wool for being soft and quiet. Thinsulate® is another fabric that is both warm and quiet, according to friends who have worn garments made of this material. Most of my sweatshirts are some type of cotton blend, and I wear them often when hunting rabbits and hares. Cotton/polyester blend shirts and coveralls or jumpsuits are my choice for hunting in warm weather. As mentioned at the outset, jeans are popular pants for use in warm to cool weather. Bib overalls are another choice.

One situation where nylon can be a good choice for rabbit hunting is when working through briars and brambles bearing thorns. Nylon-faced pants will help fend them off; nylon chaps worn over jeans will serve the same purpose. Canvas pants are another alternative.

Camouflage clothing isn't necessary for rabbit and hare hunting, but it may increase the stand hunter's and tracker's chances of success. There is a greater

Mark Eby looks for another hare to try for with handgun while dressed in camo outfit, orange hat, and Sorel boots. Camo isn't necessary for rabbit and hare hunting, but it can be beneficial when practicing certain techniques such as still-hunting and hunting from a stand.

selection of camo patterns available in hunting clothing than ever before. They come in greens, browns, grays, and whites to fit the time of year and the surroundings hunters find themselves in. An alternative to white camo for winter hunting is white coveralls. Be sure to obtain outer layers in large enough sizes so they will fit comfortably over all other layers.

Consider your state's or province's orange garment requirements for hunting before going afield with full camouflage. Bowhunters usually don't have to wear any orange, but gun hunters do in many cases. In Michigan, a hunter can conform to the rules by wearing an orange hat, but be otherwise camouflaged.

Under warmer conditions when temperatures are in the 50s and 60s, I often wear a short-sleeved tee-shirt under a long-sleeve shirt. When early-morning and evening temperatures start registering in the 40s regularly, I begin wearing long underwear, both on top and bottom, for hunting. I wear jeans and long johns until temperatures routinely drop below freezing and snow arrives, then switch to wool pants over long underwear.

Three layers on top are standard for me when temperatures are in the 40s and 50s — a light wool jacket over a larger-than-normal wool shirt untucked, and a sweater or a sweatshirt. Another layer is added for colder weather, and I often wear five layers on top for temperatures that dip as low as zero or below, with shirts, sweaters and sweatshirts under a medium-weight wool coat. A pair of jeans or a second pair of long underwear goes on under wool pants for the coldest conditions. I have hunted in below-zero weather and know what it takes to keep me warm, even if I'm moving some of the time.

Vests or coats that have game pouches in the back, plus plenty of pockets or elastic shell holders for carrying extra shotgun or rifle shells, are excellent to wear on rabbit and hare hunts. Bagged game can be carried in pouches. If your coat or vest doesn't have space for rabbits, consider carrying a shoulder bag for that purpose. Some of these bags have separators and are well suited for holding extra shells, too. Backpacks will also serve to carry the day's bag.

Choice of long underwear is a matter of personal preference. I recently tried a set that is made primarily of polypropylene and like them better than the cotton/polyester blend types I normally wear. Polypropylene is light, fits snug, and allows the evaporation of perspiration without chilling. Both fishnet and insulated long underwear are also available. One-piece

Small backpacks can come in handy for carrying extra clothing layers, as well as bagged game and accessories.

long underwear is normally warmer than two-piece sets.

Quality boots are as important for comfortable rabbit and hare hunting as clothing. Hunters with cold feet will feel cold even though their body may be adequately insulated. Leather boots are a good choice for hunting in areas where the ground is dry. Rubber boots are best for hunting where there's water and in light snow when temperatures are near freezing or warmer. Most rubber boots don't keep feet warm in cold weather, even the insulated variety. They are made in several heights. Hip boots may even be called for when hunting exceptionally wet areas for swamp or marsh rabbits.

L. L. Bean boots with rubber bottoms and leather tops are excellent footwear for all-around use during early fall. Similar boots of the Sorel variety are among the best for cold-weather use. Sorels have rubber bottoms and leather tops like Bean

Bunny boots in black are designed for comfort in extremely cold temperatures. They also come in white. Note vent above heel for blowing in air.

boots, but stand higher and include felt liners. The felt liners absorb moisture from feet, so they should be removed from boots at the end of the day to dry. Wet liners won't keep feet as warm as dry ones. A spare pair of liners ensures that a dry set will be available from one day to the next.

The warmest boots of all are appropriately named bunny boots. These heavy rubber boots have vents for blowing in air for insulation, and they come in white and black. The trade name is BATA and they can be purchased at Army-Navy surplus stores. Bunny boots are expensive, but they are worth the price to keep feet warm when temperatures dip below zero.

I usually purchase cold-weather boots at least one size larger than street shoes. This allows me to wear two or three pairs of heavy socks for added warmth.

Since the uncovered head radiates a lot of heat, it is important that your noggin be covered in cold weather. I wear either a Jones-style hat or a wool pullover watch-cap. The former is warmer and helps shade the eyes when the sun is shining. The pullover types of head coverings have a tendency to snag on branches and brush. There are a number of other types of hats that would serve the purpose just as well. Cowboy hats with wide brims are popular in the West. Hats or caps with porous

Snowshoes are a must for hunting in deep snow. This pair is narrow for comfortable walking. The webbing is neoprene, which is better than leather. Also note wool pullover headgear.

coverings are the best choices for warm-weather use.

For gloves, try not to wear types that restrict gun- or bow-handling ability. Because I find mittens too restrictive, I don't wear them. My hands are usually covered with brown cotton gloves, when it's cold enough. I can feel my gun almost as well with these light gloves on as with bare hands. In snow, cotton gloves sometimes

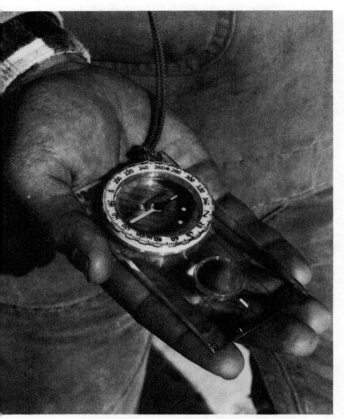

Always carry a compass when hunting rabbits and hares.

get wet, so I try to carry an extra pair.

I always wear a belt to hold my pants up and to carry a sheath knife. Some hunters prefer suspenders on their pants and carry knives in their pockets. Other items rabbit hunters should carry with them are a compass (always), extra shells, waterproof matches, tissue, lunch or high-energy snacks such as candy or raisins, and a plastic bag or two to put dressed rabbits in. A camera and extra film are optional but can really come in handy for recording memorable moments in the field. Photos taken during a hunt are always better than those back at the car or in the back yard.

You'll need snowshoes if hunting in snow that is 8 to 10 inches or more in depth. They will make walking easier, enabling hunters to cover more ground without getting worn out. Try walking a mile in 10 to 12 inches of snow without webs and a mile with them, and you'll appreciate the difference.

Snowshoes come in various sizes and styles, each rated for the amount of weight they are designed to support. I like narrow shoes, medium in length with up-turned toes. Narrow shoes enable me to walk comfortably without tripping and are still maneuverable in thick cover. The upturned toes ride over obstacles in and on the snow rather than catching on them, and prevent accumulations of snow from building up.

Neoprene webbing and harnesses are far superior to leather. For a pamphlet showing various sizes, shapes, and styles of neoprene snowshoes, write to the Iverson Snowshoe Company, Box 85, Maple St., Shingleton, MI 49884.

9

Rabbit and Hare Dogs

One of the best rabbit and hare dogs I've had the pleasure of hunting with is, believe it or not, a cocker spaniel. The dog was owned by brothers Fred and Tom DeRocher. They didn't even train the pooch; it just took to trailing rabbits and hares on its own. Tom said he took Buster for a walk one day and the dog started driving a rabbit. No one believed Tom when he told them about the dog's performance, but Buster eventually proved himself as a first-rate rabbit dog. Snowshoe hares were actually the dog's specialty, but he chased cottontails, too.

From what I remember of Buster on weekend hunts for hares years ago, he was slow and steady on a track. Bunnies that were ahead of him were seldom in a hurry, and many times they weren't far ahead of him either. The snowshoes Buster was on would run a little way and stop at regular intervals, giving hunters plenty of time for shots at them.

If a hare managed to sneak by a hunter unseen or if shots directed at it missed, it was no problem. Buster usually stuck with the trail of a snowshoe until somebody got it. Buster did have one problem: because of his long hair, balls of snow and ice would form on his feet and in his coat.

Buster was a unique dog, of course. Cocker spaniels aren't known for their ability to bark on the trail of rabbits and hares, driving them into waiting hunters. Neither are Irish setters, but my friend Ted Nugent of rock and roll fame has a setter (Paco) he says will double as a hound when not after birds. I mention these examples to illustrate that it is sometimes difficult to know what dog breed will perform well on rabbits and hares.

Dogs don't have to be bred for this type

of hunting to perform well at it. They don't even have to be a recognizable breed to be good hunters. Even mongrels can be and are used for hunting rabbits and hares. I firmly believe that with a little instinct and a lot of encouragement any dog will do what its master wants, to the best of its ability. Sometimes no encouragement is required at all, as in Buster's case. If you had a preconceived idea of what is and isn't a rabbit dog when you started reading this, I hope the above examples have broadened your outlook a little. Sometimes hunters should pay more attention to what their dogs try to show and tell them than vice versa.

Beagles are the most popular breed of hunting dog for both rabbits and hares. This trio gives a general idea of their size variation and coloration. (Photo by Wisconsin Department of Natural Resources)

There's no question that beagles are the most popular dogs for hunting rabbits and hares in North America, and they probably always will be. However, it is also a well-known fact that not all beagles make good hunters. Some of the best hunting traits have been bred out of these small hounds used for field trials, at least a portion of the dogs.

Nonetheless, I'm of the opinion that the training, encouragement, and experience any beagle gets as a pup will go a long way toward determining the hound's ultimate performance. Once a bond is developed between hunter and hound, the dog will do what it is encouraged to do to please its master, as well as following its instincts. The same is true for all dogs, not just beagles.

To increase the chances of getting a beagle that is from hunting stock, seek out breeders who are hunters themselves. Expect to pay a good price for a quality dog. Bargain-priced beagles that may also be good hunters can sometimes be obtained through classified ads in newspapers or from the local dog pound.

If you're lucky, you may even be able to get a good rabbit dog free. More than one hound that its original owner thought was useless as a hunter has proven to be a winner when handled by a person with more patience and perhaps a different approach to training or attitude about performance. Some hunters expect more from their dogs than others, sometimes more than the dogs are capable of delivering, especially in a short period of time. Rabbit dogs vary in their development as hunters. Some are quick starters and others take a little longer to catch on to what is expected of them.

The United Gundog Beagle Federation has members who breed beagles that come

Beagles can't get around in deep snow as well as bigger hounds, but this isn't as important a consideration as some hunters believe. While this beagle may appear to be swimming in deep snow, it was actually doing just fine. Deep snow will slow down some fast dogs to a more desirable speed.

from topnotch hunting stock. For information on obtaining a good hound of this breed, write or call George Pirman at 9814 Bitten Road, Bitten, MI 48116 (313-227-2238). If you write, include a stamped, self-addressed envelope for a reply.

Keep in mind that beagles come in two basic sizes: 13 and 15 inches, measured at the shoulder. Thirteen-inch beagles can actually be 13 inches or less and 15-inchers are between 13 and 15 inches. The smaller the dog, the easier it can be to care for; they don't eat as much or take up as much space. However, all beagles are basically small dogs, which makes the entire breed easier to handle, feed, and care for than larger dogs.

Beagles are good all-around rabbit and hare dogs that perform equally well on cottontails and hares. They have their limitations in deep-snow country, but it's usually possible to work around that. A pair of beagles Uncle George owned— Sammy (short for Samantha) and Scooter—were the first hounds I hunted behind. Sammy was small enough to be classed as a toy beagle, not much bigger than some of the hares she chased. As I recall, we hunted hares every weekend with those hounds regardless of the snow conditions. When the snow was deep, it simply slowed the dogs down. Even when snow was deep in the open, there was usually less in swamps, where it was sometimes packed down by hares. Both hounds were light enough to benefit from trails packed by snowshoe hares. And there were few winters that didn't have a day or two of warm weather to develop a crust on the snow solid enough to support the little dogs.

Nonetheless, a hound with longer legs than a 15-inch beagle will generally perform better in deep snow. Harriers are one possibility. These hounds, which resemble a big beagle, measure up to 21 inches high at the shoulder and weigh a minimum of 40 pounds. Harriers can be hard to find, but there is at least one contact in Michigan—John Schwartz, 17290 22 Mile Rd., Utica, MI 48087 (313/286-3674). John handles beagles as well as harriers. Always include a stamped, self-addressed envelope when writing for information.

Mixed-breed hounds can be good choices, too. Rex was a beagle/Walker cross owned by my friend Mike Hogan. In size the dog was in between both breeds (a Walker is a big hound). Rex was a terrific hare dog. I've also heard of bluetick crosses that performed well on hares, and some were no bigger than average beagles.

At the present time, George runs snowshoes with a bluetick hound. Any of the larger hound breeds such as Walkers, black-and-tans, redbones, and Plotts can make good hare hunters, with the right training. These bigger hounds, from harriers on up, are usually not well suited for chasing cottontails because of their speed. When pushed too hard, rabbits tend to hole up.

Another breed of hound that can be good on cottontails is the basset. These short-legged dogs are slow enough that there's no need to worry about them running rabbits into the ground. Bassets aren't tall (9 to 15 inches), but their bodies are chunky and they can weigh up to 70 pounds. These dogs are mild-tempered like beagles, but they can be slower learners, and they aren't designed for running

Larger hounds like this bluetick can be great on hares, but too fast for rabbits in many cases.

in more than a couple of inches of snow.

The sex of dogs doesn't matter much when it comes to their hunting ability, but it can make a difference in their association with other dogs, both at home and in the field. Some males have a tendency to fight with other males to show their dominance. However, the possibility of this trait can be reduced by hunting males with others as pups. The more males get used to associating with packmates of the same sex, especially in a hunting situation, the less likely they are to fight. Of course, if you hunt with only one dog, fighting need not be a concern.

Females will also fight with each other, but this is usually a minor problem. If females aren't spayed or if you don't plan to breed them, they must be isolated from males when in heat. Expect visits from other dogs in the neighborhood if females are kept in outside pens during these periods. Pens should be fully enclosed, both to prevent unwanted males from getting in and females from climbing out.

When trying to select a pup from a litter that might make a good hunter, take the time to watch their behavior. Those that show more aggressiveness, or curiosity, or any other traits that make them stand out from their littermates, may make the best hunters. If possible, test their reactions to a rabbit carcass or the foot of a rabbit or hare you salvaged from a kill. Any dog that shows interest in the scent of a rabbit as a pup is sure to heighten that interest with age and encouragement.

If purchasing an adult dog for hunting, try to arrange a trial run with the hound before committing yourself. Most states and provinces have provisions for training periods before hunting seasons open, when dogs can be run on rabbits as long as handlers don't carry guns. Some states

Basset hounds like this one are an option for rabbit hunting. Their short legs limit their usefulness in snow, but they work slow enough so cottontails seldom are run aground ahead of them.

allow rabbit hunting year-round, too. It is best if the dog's owner is along on runs to test the hound's performance, but if that isn't possible, make arrangements to do it yourself. This is the only way you will know for sure what you are getting into. Some dog owners have been known to exaggerate the ability of the goods, especially if they stand to profit from the transaction.

Most rabbit and hare dogs aren't ready to start hunting until they are five or six months old. However, exposure at a younger age to the game they will eventually be chasing can be a good idea. Whenever possible, present the carcass of a rabbit or hare to a pup and let the dog sniff or worry it. Reward and encourage any interest in carcasses. Let pups play with feet of rabbits and hares, too, short of eating them.

Once the pup knows what a rabbit or hare is, try laying down short scent trails with carcasses or feet, dragging them along the ground and hiding them at the end of the trail. Then start the pup at the beginning of the trail and let it try to follow the scent. Have a treat of some type handy to reward the dog if and when it finds the carcass or foot. This can be an enjoyable game for a young dog; it's also a perfect introduction to hunting on a small scale.

At the same time you are trying to interest a pup in the scent of rabbits or hares, start working on obedience training. This is something many hound hunters tend to ignore; they pay for it later when the dogs are adults. Be consistent whenever disciplining a dog. The most important word to teach a hound is "no." Use the word any time the dog does something it shouldn't, while discouraging that behavior. At the same time, encourage and reward the dog for desirable behavior of any type, whether it's in regard to housebreaking or hunting.

When a pup is old enough and big enough to follow you, take it on walks as often as possible. Every day is best, but whatever you can manage will have to do. Remember that a pup is a lot like a child. The more attention and time you give it when young, the more likely it is to develop the way you want it to. Walks don't have to be long ones, anywhere from 15 minutes to an hour is fine. Try not to wear the pup out. If it tires, wait for it to rest or carry it.

Encourage the dog's curiosity and interest in hunting as much as possible on walks, but one of the most important things to work on is getting the hound to come to you when called. When the pup is still dependent on you is the best time to do this. One way to work on the dog's response to calls is to capitalize on its urge to find you.

With this in mind, intentionally try to lose the pup on occasion, after it's accustomed to going on walks with you. Whistle to the hound with your mouth or a hand-held whistle when it starts to whine or run off in the wrong direction. Some hunters use a horn instead of a whistle. It doesn't hurt to call the dog's name after whistling or blowing a horn.

If a pup starts following your scent in an effort to find you, let it work out the trail instead of calling it. This is a good exercise for learning how to trail game. Combine the calling and scent trailing on walks at various times so a pup will benefit from both.

Some hounds, and especially beagles, are notoriously hard to catch at the end of a day of hunting. This type of training will help avoid that problem. One problem, though, is that a hound has to hear its master to be able to respond. Some dogs that are intense hunters just don't hear their masters until the rabbit they are on is shot.

While on walks with your pup keep in mind that it's a rabbit dog. If it shows any interest in chasing anything else that you don't want it to, use the word "no," and be ready to enforce it. Carry a leash with you to restrain the dog if it is inclined to disobey. Letting a dog get away with chasing something undesirable as a pup can lead to trouble later.

When it's time for a pup to start hunting, it helps to run it with an experienced dog, perhaps its mother. Experienced dogs are good teachers by simply setting good examples. They often help pups learn the tricks of the trade.

If it isn't possible to hunt a pup with a proved hound, don't hesitate to take it hunting alone. Its instincts will help it along, as will earlier exposure to rabbit scent, which you should have tried to provide. Through trial and error, the dog will eventually catch on, if the interest is there. When starting a pup on its own, you can serve as a teacher, if fresh snow is present. Go with the dog, putting it on fresh tracks that are encountered; stay with it to make sure the hound stays on the tracks, if it's having trouble.

The main thrust of these training sessions is to do just that—train the dog to chase rabbits or hares. Don't expect fantastic results right away, and be willing to sacrifice chances at rabbits. There will be plenty of time for shooting once your hunting partner knows what he's doing.

The absolute best way to start a pup is to have it actually jump a rabbit, see it run off, then be able to chase it. Try to select locations where there is a chance of this happening, both during training sessions before hunting seasons start and when actually hunting. If you see a rabbit or hare the dog doesn't, call it to the spot where the animal was seen, to start a chase.

Don't spare the praise when you bag the first rabbit or hare in front of a dog. Make a big deal about it so the hound knows it has done something good. Leave the bunny where it fell so the dog knows the chase came to a successful conclusion. It's also a good idea to have a treat along to reward the dog on the first few kills so there's no question in the pup's mind that it's doing things right.

Since rabbits and hares are often shot ahead of dogs, the sound of shots doesn't usually scare hounds. Some rabbit dogs have been known to be gun-shy, though. So it doesn't hurt to try to get a hound used to loud noises during training sessions. Associate loud noises with food, if possible, by clapping hands together loudly when it's time to eat or the dog is busy eating. When in the field, fire a .22 occasionally as the dog follows a scent or is otherwise distracted. If a pup shows fear of loud noises, make a point to spend a lot of time working on this until it gets used to them.

If there are deer in the areas where you will be running your dog on rabbits and hares, which is often the case, try to incorporate measures in training sessions to discourage the hound from running deer. Whenever possible take the opportunity to expose a rabbit dog to deer scent, with the dog on a leash for control. Repeat the word "no" while it is smelling the scent, then pull it away. If a hound shows any interest in deer scent while on its own, catch it right away and make sure it gets the idea it isn't supposed to follow that scent.

The same holds when a dog actually starts chasing a deer. Cut the chase as short as possible. If the hound breaks away from the deer when called, don't punish it—the dog may think it's being punished for coming when called.

Some houndmen use a shocking collar to break dogs on deer, and others use strong liquid scent that is supposed to sour hounds with continued exposure. Whatever training methods are used, try to be consistent. If a dog gets away with something once, it may try it again. The key is to spend as much time with a pup as possible when young, when the chances of it learning what you want and how to perform up to your expectations are best.

A healthy dog is bound to be a better hunter and will be with you for more years than one that isn't cared for properly. Be sure to get all the necessary vaccinations against rabies, parvo virus, and others your vet recommends as soon as possible. Pups are especially susceptible to parvo. If someone tells you a pup you purchase has already had its shots, ask to see proof. Also have stool samples from your dog checked regularly for parasites and administer the appropriate treatment if they are found.

Some rabbit and hare hunters have a bad habit of feeding raw bunnies to their dogs. This is a sure way to keep them infested with tapeworms, reducing their health. Tapeworm cysts are common in all rabbits and hares, sometime in muscles. If rabbits are fed to hounds, the meat should be boiled first to kill parasites. Dogs should never be permitted to eat entrails from rabbits and hares.

Heartworm, which is transmitted by mosquitoes, is a severe problem in parts of the United States, especially in southern states. Get the proper medication to protect your dog from heartworm, if it has been reported in your area.

There's a lot of responsibility associated with having a rabbit dog. Hunters who are willing to accept that responsibility and spend time working with their dogs are sure to have terrific hunting companions and enjoy plenty of action-packed days afield after rabbits and hares. Hunting with hounds is the *only way* to hunt these small game animals, as far as some hunters are concerned; after you have a dog of your own you'll be better able to understand why.

10

Hunting with Hounds

Some of my most memorable hunts for hares and rabbits have been with hounds, or at least dogs that behaved like hounds. I bagged my first rabbits and hares ahead of dogs, plus many more since then, and I hope to reap further benefits from future association with hounds in rabbit and hare habitat.

Digging deep into my memory banks, I remember one particular rabbit that made circle after circle around the same short route ahead of Sammy and Scooter, refusing to change course even though I took one or two shots at it each time it circled past my position. On the fourth or fifth circle, one of my shots finally connected. I got the impression that if I hadn't scored, that bunny would have continued its circuit until I ran out of shells or the dogs got dizzy from running in circles.

I remember another time when I, still a youngster, went hunting with three or four

adults and two dogs. I could do nothing wrong that day. It seemed as though every time the dog started a hare, the jack came my way. When we left the swamp, I had my limit of five snowshoes and my elders were emptyhanded.

On a more recent hunt with Uncle George and his son Craig, I missed five shots at a single hare before it ran into George—who bagged it. This was Craig's first hunt for hares. He was actually too young for hunting, but proud to be tagging along with his father.

Josephine, a bluetick hound, made a couple of loops through a swamp behind a snowshoe. I finally intercepted the bunny in a small clearing no more than 10 to 15 yards across, surrounded by dense young cedars. Visibility was poor. I saw the hare hopping toward me just before it hit the opening. It stopped directly behind the biggest aspen tree around as I slid my 12-

Beagle following rabbit tracks in the snow — the joy of many rabbit and hare hunters.

gauge pump gun to my shoulder. The range was about 30 feet.

A full minute or two went by as I tried to anticipate which side of the tree the snowshoe would appear on. That's a long time when you're expecting action any second. I was about to peek around the tree when the jack took a gigantic leap to the right.

Bang, bang, bang! That emptied my gun. The hare doubled back the way it had come but soon realized the dog was rapidly approaching from that direction. I barely had time to reload when the snowshoe came bounding back at me. After our previous encounter it apparently figured it had less to fear from me than from Josie. Even though the jack saw me raise the shotgun again it kept coming, approaching to within 10 feet before dodging

to the side. The snowshoe, obviously not worried, was moving at an easy stride rather than the blurring run they are capable of when scared.

Two more rounds were fired harmlessly into the snow.

When I heard George shoot and the dog stop driving, I figured he connected and headed his way. When I was almost there, Craig hollered, "Did you get one, Richard?"

"No."

Then Craig turned to his father and said, "Dad, that must have been somebody else that shot." As if 'Ol Deadeye never misses. I corrected him with a chuckle. Kids say the cutest things.

There's nothing really complicated about hunting rabbits and hares with hounds (except hitting your targets), especially if one or two good dogs are involved. The hunters' basic responsibility is to position themselves where they think the odds of seeing bunnies are in their favor, and connecting when the critters come along ahead of hounds. It may sound simple, and sometimes it is, but not always.

The best dogs will do most of the work. They will search out fresh rabbit scent once they are released, and stay on the trail of their quarry until someone gets it. Then they'll go find another rabbit or hare to chase.

We've always had our best luck, whether hunting cottontails or snowshoes, by positioning hunters in strategic locations first, just like on a drive, then having handlers and their hounds start toward hunters already in place. This increases our chances of getting fast action. If everyone starts into a piece of cover together, bunnies that are jumped quickly may make a circle or two before anyone can come close to intercepting them. When some hunters in the party are pre-positioned, they generally won't have to move far, if at all, to catch a glimpse of the first animals jumped. Even if they don't see the rabbit or hare the hounds are actually chasing, there's potential for seeing strays or sneakers that move out when the dogs first open up on a hot trail. In areas where bunnies are abundant, many of the sightings are of strays.

When chased, rabbits and hares normally run to or through the same general areas. So we usually know where to wait for the hunt to begin when hunting a location that is familiar to us. In new spots, standers should pick a position that looks promising within a reasonable distance of where the dogs are to be started. Once the

Although most rabbits and hares circle ahead of dogs, some of them, like this cottontail bagged by Pete Petosky, head across openings for new cover. (Photo by Michigan Department of Natural Resources)

Beagles are often better dogs on European hares than bigger hounds because they don't push the long-winded hares as far or as fast. Here, Major sniffs the scent in tracks in Ontario.

hunt begins and a chase starts, they are better able to determine what direction to move, if a shift in position is called for.

Even though dog handlers start after others in the party are in place, that doesn't mean they are at a disadvantage when it comes to getting in on the action. As they move with their dogs, handlers are in the best position to see or hear where rabbits and hares are jumped. Since bunnies often circle, waiting where one of them was started can be the best spot of all.

Most rabbits and hares circle, but not all of them. Some cottontails will leave a patch of cover entirely, cutting across an open field or along a fencerow to a new hideout. Snowshoe and European hares will sometimes run a straight line or follow an irregular course during the first part of the chase before settling down into a somewhat predictable running pattern. European hares can be especially long-winded if pushed hard by fast dogs, going

for miles in one direction. That's why Fred Bruins of Ontario prefers to use slow beagles rather than big hounds, so the hares don't leave the country. He said that once the big jacks get out ahead of a dog, they start circling.

Hares will also make bigger circles than cottontails, so don't be too quick to follow after the chase. About the time you start moving toward the sound of baying dogs, the hare may just begin heading back to where it started. By listening closely to dogs, it's usually possible to determine if the rabbits or hares are moving in a circle or erratically. Pick out prominent landmarks to help you judge the dogs' direction of travel; note which way they are moving in relationship to the landmark. The sound of barking will become louder as the chase comes closer, fainter as it moves away.

The volume of hounds' voices can be deceiving on days when trees and bushes are coated with snow. The walls of snow have a muting effect, and dogs often sound farther away than they actually are.

Whenever a chase is moving in a circular pattern nearby, it's often better to be patient and remain where you are; your chances of seeing game are best when you are motionless, because that's when you can best spot any movement. Rabbits and hares have excellent hearing and eyesight. They will detect your position and avoid you if you're moving. If the hounds continue to circle out of sight, move just far enough to put yourself in a better position for a shot. Wait until the dogs have passed by you and are starting another circle away from you before making your move, to reduce the chances of spooking the rabbit or hare they are chasing.

If there's snow on the ground and you come to the dog's tracks, you'll know where they've been circling. Wait nearby where visibility is best to ambush the bunny on its next go-round. Sometimes it's easier to see from a kneeling position, looking under branches rather than through them. Other times a stump, log, or knoll will serve as a good perch to give you better visibility. Be ready and looking long before the dogs get close because some rabbits and hares stay way ahead of their pursuers. Hunters who don't pay attention until hounds are almost on top of them will miss seeing lots of hares.

There's always the possibility of seeing strays regardless of where the dogs are. Movement of the hounds and of other hunters will keep local rabbits on the move. When watching for rabbits and hares, don't just look in the direction of dogs. Keep an eye peeled to the sides, too, because it's always hard to anticipate where they will appear. While you're waiting for hounds to bring a hare around, keep noise and movement to a minimum.

With a stray in the bag, I wait for a chance at the hare my dog is actually driving. When rabbits and hares are abundant, strays or sneakers will often be seen.

When shot at and missed, bunnies may still circle as they have previously, like that rabbit I eventually shot years ago. However, they will change running patterns just as often as they don't. When this happens, shifting positions again may be necessary to make another intercept. When moving or shooting, always be mindful of other hunters' positions. It's better to pass up a shot if there's even a chance it might endanger a party member. *Never shoot* when you *know* a partner is in the line of fire. If you blunder into someone else when you're moving, hustle out of their way as quickly as possible and give them plenty of space. Some groups require their members to remain at predetermined locations when hunting small covers to avoid confusion and reduce the chances of accidents.

In the event a chase goes out of hearing, there are several ways to renew contact. One option is to take a compass reading on the location where the dogs went out of hearing and follow that heading until you hear the hounds again. (It's always a good idea to take a compass reading before leaving the road at the beginning of a hunt, too, to make sure you'll know which direction to go to return to the vehicle at the end of the day.)

If there's snow on the ground when contact is lost with dogs, go to where they were last heard and pick up their tracks. Follow their trail until you're getting close once again. If you're familiar with the country and there's a road in the direction the hounds are headed, it may be possible to get ahead of them again by returning to the vehicle and driving around.

While hunting with hounds, try to keep tabs on fresh rabbit and hare sign. Then when you or someone nearby bags the bunny that the dogs were on, they can be started on another chase without much of a lull in the action.

If you think you hit a rabbit or hare that doesn't go down, or you find hair to confirm a hit that wasn't immediately fatal, mark the spot where it was last seen and put a dog on its trail, if one isn't already. A wounded bunny that is caught by a hound will often squeal or scream, and the hunter should go to the sound to retrieve it. A chase that ends abruptly is a sign the rabbit was found dead. Some dogs will retrieve hares they catch or find

On occasion, two and sometimes three snowshoes will be ahead of a hound at the same time.

dead. More often, though, hounds will try to eat their find or just leave it to go look for a live rabbit to chase.

When a stray is wounded and there's snow present, a hunter can follow up his shot by trailing the bunny himself. It doesn't take much lead to put rabbits and hares down for keeps, with the exception of the large European hares. For this reason, most rabbits that are hit solidly, even with a couple of pellets, can be recovered without much effort.

Occasionally, as many as two or three rabbits or hares may be directly ahead of hounds, especially where the game animals are abundant. Hunters should be ready in case they get the opportunity to cash in on such an occurrence. One winter day I saw three hares cross a swamp trail, one right after the other as if they were playing follow-the-leader, ahead of Scooter. I never got a shot because they were out of my range; even if I had been close enough I might not have shot; because that was the first time I saw a multiple crossing and I wasn't expecting it.

There wasn't much time to shoot anyway, because they leaped right across the trail. Both rabbits and hares have a tendency to stop on the edge of openings, then cross them as quickly as possible. For this reason, hunters watching open lanes should try to get a shot as bunnies approach the edge, or be ready for snap shooting as they cross.

Since I saw that triple-header ahead of Scooter, I have managed two doubles. The first double was a big surprise to both me and my partners, but happened so smoothly it was like an everyday occurrence. As the beagles approached my position on the edge of a swamp, a hare hopped into view from right to left and I rolled it. I had no more than worked the slide action on my pump when a second snowshoe came into view following the same course. It was as if I was shooting at the same hare all over again. The shots were so close together George and brother Bruce thought they were directed at the same snow jack. They were surprised when we met shortly afterward and they saw I had two instead of one.

My second double happened a little differently. A snowshoe ran across in front of me about 30 yards out, then stopped behind a tree out of sight. Seconds later, number two came directly toward me at closer range. I tumbled that one in its tracks and jacked in another shell in time to send a load of 6s after the first hare on the run, connecting once again.

When you're carrying a .22 rifle or handgun on hunts with hounds, rabbits or hares on the move can sometimes be stopped for a sitting shot with a sharp whistle. A shot directed at them sometimes has the same effect, so if the bullet misses, be ready for a quick followup. On the other hand, a missed shot sometimes just makes them run faster, too.

It's always a good rule to make sure of your target before you shoot. When you're hunting rabbits and hares ahead of dogs, it's especially important. Many rabbit dogs are similar in color, if not the same, as the game they are chasing. They can easily be mistaken for game when running in thick cover where only flashes of color or movement are visible. *Never* shoot at mere movements or noises. Some dogs run silently, at least for brief periods of time, and they run fast, so a hound that barks in one spot can be 20 or 30 yards away seconds later, perhaps in a completely different direction. Some rabbit dogs have been shot by careless hunters who didn't take the time to identify their intended target before shooting.

Good hounds are capable of running rabbits and hares under a variety of conditions, but certain times and conditions are better than others for this type of hunting. Dry ground holds scent poorly. Add moisture such as dew or a light rain and conditions improve dramatically. Scenting conditions are generally better in wet than dry snow, too. Neither hot nor cold weather in the extreme is well suited for running dogs.

When the weather is warm to hot, try to hunt during the coolest times of day. On days when the thermometer reaches zero or below, it's better to let temperatures warm up before hunting. Cottontails are generally not very active when it's colder than 10 to 20 degrees F. They don't move much on windy days during the winter, either. The sun and its radiating warmth bring rabbits out in force after a cold snap.

Hares are always available to chase with hounds regardless of the temperature and weather conditions, which makes them a popular choice among dogmen. However, even on days when conditions seem ideal for holding scent, the best of hounds have difficulty following tracks that are minutes old. At other times when conditions appear lousy, dogs end up trailing all day long. I mention this only to point out there's still guesswork involved in determining the best times to hunt with hounds. My advice is to hunt whenever you can that the weather is bearable for both you and your dogs.

11

In Memory of . . .

It's difficult to hunt with hounds weekend after weekend, year after year, without growing attached to them, even if they don't belong to you. That's the way it was with Sammy and Scooter.

I remember my uncle's pair of beagles fondly. They were the first rabbit dogs I hunted with. Actually, there was a little more to our association than just hunting. George's job took him out of town occasionally, and I sometimes took care of the dogs while he was gone. I knew the little dogs almost as well as George because, like him, I saw them develop from pups into hunters, tagging along on preseason training runs where they learned how to unravel scent trails left by both cottontails and snowshoe hares. It was also good training for me to learn how to ambush bunnies ahead of the dogs. Sammy and Scooter and I grew into rabbit hunters together.

The two dogs were quite a pair. Scooter was the typical beagle, white with black and brown patches on her back, and of average size. Sammy was smaller, barely bigger than some of the hares she chased, and her coat was white and brown, no black. Since they always hunted together, they often teamed up on the same scent.

They both knew how to use their noses but when together, they seemed to work as one dog—Scooter was the nose and Sammy the mouth. For such a small dog, Sam had a terrific voice, a loud, clear bawl that carried a long way. Scooter never developed much of a voice, maybe because she learned to rely on Sam's. The bigger dog was often silent when they ran together. If Scooter did open her mouth,

Sammy leads the way out of a swamp. Owner George Smith follows, carrying a pair of snowshoe he got ahead of the dog during her last hunting season.

you knew she was practically on top of the rabbit or hare she was chasing. She never did bark, though; a series of high-pitched yips or squeals came out of her mouth when she was hot on a hare.

Despite Sam's size, it seemed as though she thought she was the toughest dog around. She frequently started fights with dogs much bigger, or at least acted as though she wanted to, but no serious altercation developed that I can recall. Sammy and Scooter did their share of fighting between themselves, but no real harm was done.

Those two beagles weren't perfect, but when it came to chasing rabbits and hares, they usually got the job done. In good areas with lots of hares, each of them often took her own track and we had two chases going at once.

George, my brother Bruce, and I shot hundreds of snowshoes ahead of those hounds. The five of us enjoyed many hunts together, but it was so long ago now that many of the details are far from fresh in my memory. Only bits and pieces come back to me, generally unusual circumstances, like the time I pulled Scooter from a stream in the winter. She had fallen in while chasing a snowshoe, and the banks were steep and high above the water, too high for her to climb out.

Sometimes we were stumbling around in the dark until we finally caught the beagles. There was even a time or two one or both dogs were out overnight. Whenever we weren't able to catch Sammy and Scooter before leaving for home, George put a blanket or coat in the woods just out of sight of the road where the vehicle had been parked or at the point where we walked out to the road. Lost dogs will frequently trail their owners to a road and lie down on something with familiar scent.

The blanket or coat trick is the recommended procedure any time you leave a hunting area without your dogs. They can usually be picked up hours later or the next morning at that spot, as Sammy and Scooter usually were. However, if at all possible, it is best to catch rabbit dogs before dark so they don't have to be left in the woods. If a dog is always tough to retrieve, it's a good idea to start trying to catch it before the last hour of daylight. Shooting a rabbit ahead of the hound and waiting to grab the stubborn pooch when it reaches the kill, is a good way to catch a dog. If that proves too time-consuming, go directly to the driving dog, anticipating its course and an intercept point.

Unfortunately, I didn't take an interest in recording our outings until Scooter was already gone. She developed a physical problem and had to be put to sleep. Sammy lived a few years longer, and I did record some events during her last hunting season. Her performance was excellent that winter, particularly on one beautiful sunny day when temperatures reached the upper 30s.

The snow was wet and held scent well. A few inches of recently fallen white stuff overlay a crust. The crust was enough to support Sammy's light weight, but George and I needed snowshoes.

Our first stop was at an evergreen swamp bordering a paved county road. We had taken hares from the spot in previous years, and a number of bunny tracks indenting the snow was enough to tell us more were available for Sam to chase. George and I worked into the swamp parallel to each other, with Sammy sniffing tracks between us. Within a matter of minutes the dog opened with one of her far reaching bawls and lit out on good scent, tonguing all the way.

We immediately took up positions that would offer each of us the best possible view of different sections of cover the snowshoe might circle back through. George carried his shotgun. If he got a chance at the hare Sam was driving he wanted to collect it, as much for the dog as himself. He knew she didn't have many more hunts ahead of her. I was toting a scoped .22 rifle, my favorite for winter hare hunting.

Excited tones of Sam's baying were coming in loud and clear. There was no difficulty keeping up with the progress of the chase. Beagle and bunny went deeper into the swamp initially, but the snowshoe eventually turned back toward us, a pattern typical of a pursued hare.

As Sam drew close I squatted down in an effort to see better. I kept swinging my head from left to right, looking for a flash of movement that might be a flexing hare. Then George shot.

"He probably got him," I thought.

I waited, expecting to hear Sammy's tonguing stop abruptly as she came upon the downed snowshoe. But she kept going, driving hard as she passed by me just out of sight.

"Hey, George," I hollered out, "did you miss that rabbit?"

"No," he answered. "I got the one I shot at, but the dog wasn't on it. Must have been a stray."

With that I adjusted my position, moving to the area the snowshoe had gone through unseen, hoping to get a crack at it the second time around. George did the same. A charge of 6s from his modified tube caught up with the pursued snowshoe as it circled again.

After a short powwow we decided to snowshoe into a section of the swamp the dog hadn't penetrated yet. Once there,

Sammy picked up another track. This chase outlasted the earlier one. The hare would make a couple of laps around one segment of the cover, then line out to a different area and start circling again. George's little beagle was staying on the critter's tail all the way. After better than two hours of this, George once again made an intercept and nailed the erratic bunny.

Sam was holding up exceptionally well considering the lack of exercise she had prior to this outing. Of course, she had easy going, consistently staying up on the crust. It must have been almost like running on bare ground, perhaps better.

After George collected that third hare we moved on to a different location. The swamp was tracked up by then. A hare was started right off the bat, once we pushed our way into a promising-looking thicket of spruce. Sam brought the snow jack around in a tight circle toward the starting point, but the chase reversed directions just short of our stands. Within minutes the hound's hardy voice had almost faded out of hearing. She stayed a good distance away for some time, so we had to move in on her. When we finally closed in, George scored for the fourth time. He had one shy of his limit and I hadn't even seen a live snowshoe.

We made another move. This time George told me to go into the cover first and pick a spot where I could see as well as possible. After ten minutes, he entered at the opposite end of the swamp with Sammy, and they moved toward me.

The spot I picked to wait for action was along the edge of two cover types, which hares frequently move through when chased. I had a good view of a thick clump of cedars to my right and a semi-open expanse of tag alders to my left.

Sammy opened up eventually and I got ready. She must have been a good hundred yards away yet when I saw movement in the alders—a snowshoe. I saw it for just a moment at a time as it flashed through small openings en route from one bit of cover to another.

The jack hadn't offered a good sitting shot by the time it got even with me and didn't look like it was going to, so I picked the hare up in the scope, trying to align the crosshairs on the moving target. I fired three shots with the semiautomatic rifle. None of them hit, and in fact they just speeded up the snowshoe's retreat. As the jack zipped into a sizable opening I rattled off three more quick ones. Just as the bunny was going out of sight, it tumbled with a hit through the heart.

That ended the day for us. It was late and Sammy was tired, but it had been a good day; we had bagged all the snowshoes Sam drove, plus one. The beagle made a few more hunts with us that season but never made it to the next. She suffered kidney failure and was put to sleep.

Another hound I didn't know, but would have liked to, is Speed. She would have been the envy of any rabbit or hare hunter, except for one trait—she was hard to catch at the end of the day. Of course, that shortcoming is common among dogs that are exceptional hunters. They get so immersed in the pursuit they don't want to quit.

Bill St. Martin from Munising, Michigan, was the proud owner of Speed, a cross between a beagle and a bluetick. When Bill got the dog as a puppy, he thought she would probably reach 14 inches when full grown, because of her parentage. She didn't. In fact, she didn't even make 12 inches.

Speed was skinny and small. Some of the hares she ran were bigger than she was, according to St. Martin. And she was fast. In view of the pace at which she chased hares through Alger County swamps, she was well named. Despite her size, Speed's voice wasn't lacking, Bill said. Her baying was loud and far-reaching when she was on the trail of a snowshoe.

Speed exhibited her enthusiasm for chasing rabbits at an early age. She was hunting at three months, when she was still so small she couldn't make it over many of the logs she encountered on the trail. "Whenever Speed came to a log she couldn't get over," St. Martin said, "she would stand there whimpering and barking until someone came. When I lifted her over, she was gone in a flash after the rabbit."

On the way to and from hunting spots, Bill carried Speed in a game pouch in the back of his hunting coat. When it was time for her to hunt, he simply opened the pocket and she jumped out. After the hunt, he leaned backwards, holding the pocket open, and she jumped back in.

The only problem was getting her to realize the hunt was over for the day. St. Martin said in desperation he finally hit upon the only thing that worked. First he would shoot the jack she was chasing; she always came up to a bunny that was shot in front of her. When she stopped, he would step on her — carefully — with a snowshoe. That's what it took to convince her it was time to go home. Nothing else worked; the little hound was fast enough to elude anyone who tried to catch her by hand.

Sometimes Speed spent days at a time chasing snowshoes. Whenever Bill couldn't catch his dog, he would call his friends and tell them where she was, if they wanted to hunt. They often succeeded in catching her on following trips.

It was on one of the times Bill couldn't catch Speed that he lost her. She had been gone for a period of three years when one day he saw her walking next to another fellow on the opposite side of the street in downtown Munising.

"Hey, Speed, what you doing over there?" he called.

The hound recognized her master, raced across the road, and jumped into his arms. The other fellow recognized that St. Martin was her original owner because of her response to his calls. Speed's temporary master had picked her up in the woods three years before, thinking she was abandoned.

It is hard to say how many snowshoe hares were shot in front of Speed, but it must have been in the thousands. St. Martin said it was nothing for him and his brothers to shoot 40 to 50 of the snow jacks off of her in a weekend of hunting. She hunted faithfully and untiringly for 17 years.

One day while hunting near a local lake, Bill shot a hare Speed was driving. He heard her bark on the snowshoe's trail, but she never came to the kill.

Bill knew something was wrong, because she had never done that before. He backtracked the rabbit and found Speed, dead in the hare's tracks. She was buried on the spot. That location was eventually cleared and a garage constructed over the dog's grave.

Speed, Sammy, and Scooter are all gone now, but their memory will live on, and so will the memories of other rabbit dogs like them across North America.

12

Try Tracking

It was snowing heavily when I turned my vehicle down a road in the woods, looking for a place to hunt snowshoe hares. I went a half mile without seeing what I was looking for, so I turned around. On the way back toward the main road I spotted a pleasing sight—fresh hare tracks.

They weren't there when I first went by, so I knew they couldn't be any more than a few minutes old. On top of that, the tracks entered a narrow patch of tag alders sandwiched between the road and a stream. The hare had to be in that patch of cover, and I figured my chances of getting a shot at it by following the bunny's tracks were terrific.

I parked the vehicle and hastily loaded my semiautomatic .22 rifle with solid long-rifle bullets. Pausing on the edge of the alders where the tracks entered, I followed the prints with my eyes as far as I could, on the chance the hare was hiding close by. It was early November, so I searched for an out-of-place patch of brown, figuring the animal wouldn't have turned white yet.

Nothing caught my eye, so I started to move into the alders. But before stepping into the cover, I decided to change tactics. I figured the snowshoe would run ahead of me as soon as I started following it and would cross the road again farther down, out of sight. The vehicle was parked next to the road where the hare entered the cover, and I reasoned that the bunny would be hesitant to recross the road there. So I walked down the road about 50 yards in the direction the hare was headed and cut into the alders going back toward where it entered, hoping it would hold its ground between me and my vehicle.

It was a good idea, but it didn't work. The snowshoe, less concerned with my rig than me, *did* recross the road. I followed the tracks slowly and quietly into a stand of evergreen trees on the opposite side of the road and was intently looking at the prints when a second hare hopped up off to the side. It ran a short distance and stopped on the opposite side of a log, with only its ears remaining in view.

I tried to maneuver into position for a shot, but it hopped away. Switching to the second animal's tracks, I pussyfooted along them, carefully looking ahead. As I stepped around a balsam fir tree, there the hare sat, preening itself, unaware of my presence. I hastily aimed for the head and shot. An unseen branch deflected the bullet. Two hops and the confused snowshoe stopped again. My second round was on target.

Spirits bolstered, I returned to the original set of tracks. That snowshoe proved too smart for me, though. I caught one glimpse of it as it raced away in high gear. The only opportunity for a shot would have been with a scattergun. The hare eventually led me into a bog where there were a number of tracks, making it difficult to stay on one set, so I left that area to look for another set of fresh tracks to follow.

One of the most exciting, challenging, and rewarding methods of hunting hares and rabbits once snow blankets the ground is tracking them one on one, hunter against animal. Some of them can be as sneaky as a big-racked white-tailed buck deer when it comes to staying out of sight of a trailing hunter. So it calls for a healthy measure of cunning on a hunter's part to score consistently when using this technique.

To be successful, hunters have to possess tracking skills, be stealthy enough to get close to the quarry in thick cover, and use their eyes to spot the critters, which are often camouflaged in their surroundings. Luck can play a role, too, of course, as it did for me when I stumbled on the second snowshoe while following another. Anything can happen when you're following in the tracks of rabbits and hares.

If you haven't already done so, refer to the chapter on sign for specific information on rabbit and hare tracks.

Hares can be relied upon to provide snowtracking opportunities consistently, regardless of the weather. Rabbits, on the other hand, hole up during cold or nasty weather; sometimes their tracks will even disappear into a hole when the pressure is on and you're close to getting a shot. However, rabbits don't normally leave a trail of tracks as long as hares do. Both cottontails and snowshoes have a tendency to circle when trailed, but jacks or European hares commonly head cross-country when jumped. Hunters tracking these latter species better be prepared for a long walk or be ready to look for another set of tracks, if they don't connect on them when first jumped.

The best times to try tracking are when snow is falling or soon after a snowfall ends. Under either circumstance it is usually easy to distinguish fresh tracks. If the accumulation of snow is heavy, fresh prints are probably the only ones that will be visible. When a light dusting of snow has fallen, indentations that have snow in them will be old, as far as the tracker is concerned, and those without snow in them will be fresh.

Although fresh snow makes tracking easier, the technique can be practiced any time there's a covering of snow on the ground. With experience, it's possible to differentiate between old and new tracks regardless of the snow conditions. On

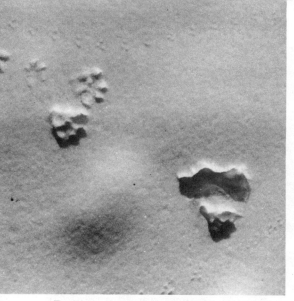

Fresh snowshoe hare track, with toeprints visible.

sunny days that warm up enough for the snow to begin melting, old prints will melt along with it and fresh ones will be unmelted. When it's windy, old tracks will soon be covered with loose snow or literally blown away, especially in open habitat such as that occupied by European and Arctic hares or jack rabbits.

There's a variety of ways to find fresh tracks initially. Driving woods roads as I was when I encountered that hot snowshoe track is one option. Snowmobiles, three-wheelers, and other all-terrain vehicles can be used to cruise lanes or trails in search of fresh spoor, too. However, foot travel may be the best way to start out such a hunt.

Rabbits or hares can't be counted on to cross roads during the middle of the day. It was fairly early in the morning when I found the hare tracks mentioned at the beginning of this chapter, although it's not always possible or practical to hunt early and late in the day. During winter months, cottontails are most active above 20 degrees Fahrenheit, and on some days that temperature range may not be reached

until midday. Even when rabbits and hares are active, they spend most of their time in protective cover and won't necessarily venture across roads or trails.

In good habitat, it doesn't usually take much effort on foot to jump a rabbit or hare and come across its trail. When looking for fresh tracks to follow I move along at a brisk pace, making no attempt to be quiet, and frequently zigzagging through patches of cover where rabbits or hares are likely to be hiding. If a good set of tracks isn't located quickly, I circle back around the edges of cover I've walked through, to pick up prints off to the sides or behind me. Rabbits and hares are notorious for circling hunters, striking out in the direction their predators came from.

Bowhunter Gene Ballew follows fresh rabbit tracks, looking carefully ahead for any signs before moving on.

Once I'm on to a set of fresh footprints I settle down to a slow and cautious pace, trying to keep noise to a minimum. The best trackers use their eyes more than their feet. Try to follow the tracks with your eyes as far as possible, closely scrutinizing potential hiding spots. Only when you're convinced the track-maker isn't in view, either ahead or to the sides, should your feet be used to move ahead.

In situations where game isn't abundant and the only tracks you've seen have snow in them, by all means follow those prints. It may take a while to catch up, especially if the animal is one of the larger species of hares, but that's part of the challenge of this type of hunting. There's always the possibility those tracks will lead you to a fresher trail.

There are a couple of reasons why I like tracking rabbits and hares. First off, I'm constantly aware of the presence of my quarry. It's out there somewhere ahead of me and may be spotted at any second, if I'm a skillful hunter. The constant possibility of pending action keeps me on my toes. I'm seldom bored while sneaking along the trail of a cottontail or snowshoe.

I also learn a lot about rabbits and hares while following in their footsteps, which interests me. It's like reading a magazine article or book. There are few tracking efforts on which I don't learn something new about the animal's behavior, feeding habits, habitat preferences, or the tricks they pull to elude their pursuers. Sometimes I'm so intent on what a rabbit or hare *did*, I'm not paying as much attention as I should to what it's *doing*. I might even miss some chances for shots, but that's part of the fascination.

Don't expect it to be easy to spot hares or rabbits you are following when they are motionless. Their presence won't always be obvious, even when you're looking directly at them, especially hares that have donned camouflage winter coats of white. Cottontails aren't slouches when it comes to hiding from view either, though. The key is not to look for the whole animal. Search for distinctive pieces of their anatomy such as an eye or ear. Those are the most prominent features on a snowshoe hare. Brown eyeballs and black-tipped ears contrast with the snow; everything else blends in.

Because of their natural camouflage, hares will sometimes stop in surprisingly open spots to wait for their pursuer. Cottontails like to duck under dried clumps of brown grass, brush, and logs or scrunch up next to a brown-trunked tree, anything that they can become a part of to reduce their visibility. The shiny eye of a cottontail can be a clue to its presence.

A trick cottontails sometimes use to become invisible is to burrow into the snow.

While following tracks, make it a practice to look ahead and to the sides for signs of the rabbit or hare you are following. Many times, just an eyeball or ears will tip you off to the location of an animal.

Tracking hunter who has spotted a hare takes careful aim with .22 rifle.

It thoroughly confuses the unindoctrinated tracker. If a cottontail's tracks end suddenly and you can't relocate them, look for a hole in the snow. If you find one, the rabbit is at the end of it. Probing the snow by the hole with a foot should prompt the bunny to show itself suddenly. Be ready to shoot!

If you're following a cottontail, it's a good idea to walk to the side of tracks so they won't be obliterated, especially if the trail should suddenly end. Hares never stoop so low to avoid detection and when trailing them I sometimes prefer to walk in their tracks, always making sure I know where the next prints are before stepping on those directly in front of me. I once followed a snowshoe that circled in the same spot three or four times. At the end it was impossible to tell which prints were the freshest. If I had stamped out each set of tracks as I followed them, that confusion would have been minimized.

Both rabbits and hares will backtrack or leap to the side where their prints aren't easy to see, so don't assume a cottontail chose to bury itself in the snow if the trail ends. Look carefully off to the sides in nearby brush opposite where tracks end. Look behind, too. Hares will hop on rocks, stumps, or logs as well as along them, and I assume cottontails occasionally do the same thing. If prints end near one of these objects and there is no snow on them, check around them to see if they were used as "stepping stones" to break the line of tracks.

Jim Carpenter from Grand Blanc, Michigan, is a master cottontail tracker; he contends that the rabbits always backtrack and leap off to the side when settling into a hideout. When you see this telltale pattern of tracks, look carefully for the cottontail that should be nearby. Jim recommends continuing to shuffle your feet while searching clumps of grass, brush, and snow for signs of the rabbit's whereabouts; the animals feel threatened when a hunter stops and may run. If you're carrying a shotgun instead of a .22, stopping and standing at ready may be the best thing to do.

To increase the odds of seeing rabbits or hares that are moving out ahead of you, it helps to screen upcoming terrain as far ahead as possible while advancing. This is assuming nearby cover has been carefully examined before you move forward. However, even if a rabbit or hare jumps close by, eyes concentrating on distant objects will still pick up the movement and your gaze can be shifted accordingly. When concentrating on cover close by, it's easy to overlook movement in the distance.

By looking ahead for moving game I don't mean just glancing directly in front of you. Remember, rabbits and hares are circlers. The critter's course may be veering to the right or left rather than straight ahead. Keep this in mind when trying to spot one sitting or streaking away.

The best way to get a look at the rabbit or hare ahead of you may not always be to remain doggedly on its tracks, as I've learned over the years. When the trail leads into a thick patch of cover ahead, it is often advisable to circle the thicket, looking for the rabbit or hare as you go, paying particular attention to the back side. Rabbits and hares frequently wait in such locations until they hear the tracker enter the patch of cover, then zip out the far side where the hunter can't possibly see them.

If you see tracks leaving the thicket, continue along them. The savings in time will put you closer to your quarry, making a shot possible very soon. If there are no prints exiting the patch of cover, the rabbit or hare must still be inside and a thorough reexamination of its interior is in order. A careful search of the contents of a thicket from along the edges will sometimes be rewarded.

To get an upper hand on circling rabbits and hares, try backtracking or cutting across the circle to intercept the unsuspecting bunny. After two or three circles are completed, hunters will have an idea how to short-circuit the next one. Keep in mind that cottontails and snowshoe hares will often circle back to the spot where they were jumped. This can help anticipate an interception.

One day while looking for a fresh set of hare tracks to follow, I jumped a snowshoe under a fallen tree. I picked up the tracks and soon realized the bunny was circling back to its form. Having an idea

where the fallen tree was, I left the hare's trail and pussyfooted toward the tree. As expected, the hare was sitting where I originally jumped it, watching its backtrack. It never knew what hit it.

Another trick to pull on unsuspecting rabbits and hares that choose to circle is to run after them when jumped, then backtrack to the starting point and wait. Patience will sometimes be rewarded by a bunny that expects you to be coming behind it, not waiting ahead of it.

Regardless of how you do it, tracking rabbits and hares can be fun and exciting, plus a learning process. For every trick you try, they have one or two of their own. All animals have their own quirks. Some can be easy to follow and get a shot at, if you are careful, while others are always a jump or two too far ahead.

Uncle George once had a snowshoe hare elude him by swimming across a river. He saw the snow jack's tracks on the opposite bank where it exited the water, but there was no way he could cross after it. The water was too deep and cold. European hares are good swimmers and won't hesitate to cross rivers and streams to shake either dogs or human trackers.

A snowshoe being tracked by brothers Jerry and Terry Weigold gets my vote for the most innovative disappearance. They followed the hare's tracks into a hollow log. Without looking inside, one of them grabbed a pole and started probing the log's interior in an attempt to push the sneaky snowshoe out into the open. What they jabbed with the pole was a hibernating black bear, not a snowshoe. The hare apparently hopped over the sleeping bruin and was hiding on the other side of it.

13

Drives

Two or more hunters can team up to increase their chances of success by conducting drives. There are two basic ways to do this.

When snow blankets the ground, one member of the party can dog individual hares or rabbits while partners try to intercept them. If there are no volunteers for playing rabbit dog, the group can be split up, with one or two members selected as drivers and the remainder serving as standers. The goal here is for the drivers to chase a number of rabbits or hares occupying a patch of cover into the standers, who do most of the shooting. This type of drive can be conducted with or without snow.

Either approach can produce desirable results. Tracking drives are essentially the same as hunting with hounds, except that in this case the dogs don't always have voices that are as good, but they can be easier to catch at the end of the day. Just kidding.

Seriously, having a hunter serve as dog has real advantages over hunting with the canine variety. Hunters on the track of rabbits or hares can bark, holler, or whistle as they are trailing, to give partners a general direction on the fleeing bunny, just like dogs. But unlike dogs they can also shout instructions that can be helpful in intercepting game, if the tracker is familiar with the hunting area and where the partners are stationed.

"Hey, Harry, he's coming your way. Get ready."

"The rabbit just turned west, headed for the fenceline."

"Pete. Go to the river crossing. That's where this one's headed!"

"I just saw him. Get ready!"

The ficticious quotes above are examples of the type of information a good human hound can relay to partners. I've never hunted with a canine that could do that. This type of added information isn't necessary, of course, but it can be helpful in some cases. Steady barks, shouts, or whistles are often enough for standers to anticipate where they might intercept rabbits or hares that are being trailed. Besides the one being followed, there's a chance others will be jumped, too, to provide shooting for standers.

The tracking drive is definitely a good option for hunters who don't have access to a rabbit dog but do have at least one hunting partner.

I well remember the first tracking drive I made for my brother and a brother-in-law, Bruce Dupras. They both seemed skeptical about my idea but indulged me. We stopped at a promising-looking spot made up of a mixture of evergreen trees, aspen, and hazel brush. I let them get in position at one end of the patch of cover, then went to the opposite end and started toward them, looking for a fresh set of tracks.

In short order I had one and announced it by hollering, "Heads up, here comes one!" It was a hare in this case and it was headed in the right direction. My bark isn't real good, so I continued voicing my progress on the track with what I thought was an appropriate tune: "She'll Be Comin' Round the Corner When She Comes." My singing isn't actually very good either, but I decided to do something different than your average hound. After all, this was a special occasion. We were trying something new.

As the tracks led me closer to my partners I heard a shot, soon followed by three

more. When Dupras came into view, I saw he had the snowshoe.

"How come it took you so many shots to get 'im?" I asked.

"I was laughing so hard at your singing, I couldn't hold the gun steady," he replied.

They weren't too impressed with my voice, but they were convinced that the technique worked after that episode. Another time brother Bruce and I teamed up with Uncle George to try some tracking drives. We headed into a stand of jack pine trees where we had met with success on previous hunts with hounds. I was content to let Bruce and George play dog, and they were in good voice, sounding every bit like experienced beagles.

This hunt was really a mixed bag of experimentation. I had my .50-caliber muzzle-loading rifle, using 80 grains of powder behind a round ball. George had a new .30-30 he wanted to try out, and Bruce brought along some .22 rimfire shotshells to test in his semiautomatic rifle.

It snowed before our arrival, so we knew any tracks we saw would be fresh. To start, we spread out in a line and walked abreast of one another until a hare was jumped. George took the track in full voice, but he waited for Bruce and me to take up stands in the direction the hare was headed first.

I eventually saw the snowshoe; it stopped about 30 yards away with just its head visible. When the smoke cleared the bunny was still sitting in the same place with its ears twitching. It vacated the premises when I started to reload.

Bruce took over the track at that point; George was next in line for a shot, but he also missed. George then resumed his role as hound and was moving toward me when a hare hopped into view and stopped in an opening. This time I took more careful aim, and connected. The round ball entered behind the right shoulder and exited the chest, leaving a clean hole.

As it turned out, the snowshoe I bagged wasn't the one George was on. It was a stray. The human hound passed by out of sight, baying steadily, and a short time later Bruce's .22 cracked twice. The next thing I knew, my brother was in full cry after the hare. He, too, had missed, as George and I did earlier. I later learned that the shotshell didn't eject from Bruce's rifle because it was too long once fired. His second shot was with a regular long rifle bullet.

The hare my partners were following was leading a charmed life, but George finally brought it to an end as the snowshoe circled ahead of Bruce. His rifle bullet just grazed the hare's head, but it did the trick nonetheless.

Silent tracking drives are an alternative to the barking, singing, hollering, whistling variety. They are a good choice for bowhunters. Under these circumstances, either the driver or standers can get shooting. Standers must constantly remain alert once a drive begins, because most of the time it is impossible to know where the rabbit or hare and the driver are.

One day I joined Dr. William Robinson for a silent tracking drive. I took the role of tracker when we hit a fresh track. We both had recurve bows. After giving Bill enough time to pick a stand, I started off along the tracks.

There wasn't much cover in the stand of hardwood trees where the prints led, so I didn't expect to jump the hare right away.

Another hint that it might travel a few hundred yards before stopping were its widely spaced tracks, indicating the snowshoe was running at a good clip through the open habitat. However, within 50 yards a hollow depression at the base of a hazel bush caught my eye.

A close look revealed two black-tipped ears and part of the body of a hiding snowshoe hare. A clump of snow suspended by several small branches blocked most of the snow jack from view. It was only 15 to 20 feet away, an excellent bow shot. If I hadn't been looking, a few more steps would have put me right on top of the sitting snowshoe.

After nocking a broadhead-tipped arrow, I eased the string of the 52-pound-pull bow back to full draw and let fly. The shaft caught a branch and zipped into the snow off target. Disturbed by the commotion, the hare hopped forward into full view but was still screened by branches.

Arrows 2, 3, and 4 met the same fate as the first. After the second shaft, the jack held its ground, obviously confused by the proceedings but certainly not worried. Arrow number 4 was my last one, so I took out my camera and "shot" the snowshoe several times before it finally scurried away toward Bill.

"Heads up, Bill," I shouted to alert my partner. "He's coming your way!"

I was surprised when I got a reply. Bill had a hard time containing his laughter as he called back, "Yeah, I know. I saw the whole thing."

My performance was certainly not intended for an audience. The lack of cover in the hardwoods provided my partner with a ringside seat to the episode. Meanwhile, the hare holed up under a lone spruce tree between us. As I retrieved a

Dr. William Robinson holds up hare he bagged with arrow after watching me empty my quiver at it.

However, safety is of utmost importance on a drive, and all hunters should take only shots that do not endanger party members. Some groups of hunters who regularly drive rabbits and hares prohibit drivers from carrying guns. Drivers and standers routinely alternate so everyone gets in on the action. To increase visibility to one another, hunters participating in drives should wear bright-colored upper garments or vests, preferably orange. In fact, this is a good idea at all times when hunting rabbits and hares, and is mandatory in many states.

Although more than one driver can be used, if the cover is small to moderate sized, one is often enough, leaving others in the party to take stands. As with tracking drives, two hunters is the minimum number required to make regular drives work. It worked for Wayne Van Zwoll and me on cottontails in Kansas.

couple of my arrows, Bill moved into position for a shot and scored.

Regular drives are conducted much the same as tracking drives, only the objective is to push more than one rabbit or hare toward standers. There can be more than one driver, and snow doesn't have to be present. The principle is simple. Pick a patch of cover limited in size and with well-defined borders created by roads, railroad or power line rights of way, fields, rivers, lakes, and more. Then position standers in appropriate spots — at one end or in openings near heavy cover. If trails made by rabbits or hares are visible, posting in view of these is a good choice.

Both drivers and standers may get shots at rabbits and hares that are jumped.

With one rabbit to his credit, Wayne Van Zwoll waits for another on a drive of weed patch.

Wayne Van Zwoll remains ready in the background for another cottontail to hop into the open on drive.

We were hunting a 2- or 3-acre weed patch, longer than it was wide, with roads at both ends and open fields on both sides. Wayne used a bolt action .22 mounted with a 4-power scope. Rather than trying to drive the whole patch at once, we broke it up into sections, with Wayne positioning himself in openings where he was likely to see rabbits. And see rabbits he did.

An exact count of sightings was impossible, but by the time we were done, Wayne saw at least 20 cottontails that I pushed past him, and I saw others that snuck around behind me, refusing to go the way I wanted them to. On one drive Wayne head-shot a rabbit, plus missed another, and on the final push nailed a pair of cottontails. He was very selective about the shots he took, too. He saw rabbits on every drive, most of which simply didn't provide good rifle shots. With a shotgun, Wayne could have really cleaned up, probably bagging his daily limit of ten with ease.

Drives are an excellent technique for cashing in on both white-tailed and black-tailed jacks during winter months when they often concentrate in small patches of cover such as shelter belts. This is a favored tactic used by fellow writer and photographer Ron Spomer. He said jacks will leave shelter belts in any direction, so standers cover as many sides as possible while a driver walks through the cover. Ron recalled one memorable day he dropped nine white-tailed jacks in about two minutes with a Browning .22 rimfire auto-loader.

"I positioned myself in a scattering of trees along a creek which just happened to be the resident jacks' favorite escape route," Ron said. "A partner walks into the day roost—a shelter belt—and rousts

Don Lowin (*left*) and Bob Spomer with collection of white-tailed jacks taken on a drive in South Dakota. (Photo by Ron Spomer)

them out. Minutes later, I am being swarmed by fifty or eighty hares. After emptying my twenty-two, I take out the pistol, sit real still, and pick my shots as the seemingly blind jacks hop within ten yards."

This is an example of how much action is possible on drives for jacks when the animals are concentrated in small patches of cover. All drives won't be as productive as the one Ron mentioned, of course. Sometimes the hares get the upper hand, and most of them get safely by standers. When making a drive in a location for the first time, it may be difficult to determine which way these hares will run when jumped and to intercept them, especially if there are a limited number of standers. In the event many jacks escape without providing shooting, keep their escape route in mind for the future. They will often flee in the same direction on subsequent drives.

Large-scale drives or roundups are sometimes used to help control black-tailed and white-tailed jack numbers when their populations explode. These are not sporting events, but economic necessities for farmers in affected areas. I mention these drives in concluding this chapter to illustrate how abundant jacks can sometimes become and what impact they can have when they reach these extremes.

During population explosions jacks eventually exhaust their natural food supply, then turn to farmers' crops, causing huge financial losses. These periodic large-scale drives help reduce losses.

The last peak year for blacktails in Idaho was 1981–82. More than 100,000 jacks were killed on drives during 1982 in Idaho. By mid-January of 1982, farmers near the small town of Mud Lake estimated their losses of hay and grain to these hares at more than $10 million. At normal population levels, jacks cause a minimum of damage and are tolerable, but when they number in the hundreds of thousands, something has to be done to salvage crops.

Preceding drives, a specified area is fenced, leaving an opening or gate. Wing fences are then set up at angles away from each side of the gate, forming a funnel. A large number of drivers herd jacks into the enclosure, where they are killed.

These roundups have been conducted in the West for over 100 years. In Idaho, Utah, Oregon, and Colorado the recorded tally of jacks taken on 220 drives between 1875 and 1895 was 470,000. A reported 370,000 hares were chalked up on 155 drives in California between 1888 and 1895.

The fact that jacks are capable of damage resulting in large economic losses to farmers is one reason they can be hunted year-round in many western states. This works to the advantage of hunters because they can conduct drives of their own any time of the year, although winter is often best. In addition, hunters interested in trying for jacks on farmland, where the animals are often abundant, shouldn't have any difficulty obtaining permission from farmers.

14

Jump Shooting

Jim Haveman and I were actually pheasant hunting, but we got into cottontails. I had shot the cottony-tailed rabbits in front of beagles and while tracking before, but this was my first experience jump shooting them, and I learned a valuable lesson. Shooting them is different than snowshoe hares, which I was more familiar with.

My partner and I walked side by side through fields filled with weeds and along the edges of thick patches of cover consisting of brush and young trees. Along the edges of the fields and brush, we jumped the rabbits. I put up the first one and was amazed at its running speed. A snap shot missed.

The next cottontail bounced up in front of Jim. He's an old hand at busting these bunnies, and an excellent shotgunner besides, so the result of his shot was predictable.

Rabbit number 3 is the one that taught me a lesson I'll never forget. Jim jumped it, and called out, "Hey, Rich, there's another cottontail. Comin' your way."

Forewarned, I was ready when this rabbit hopped into view. Then it stopped. We had talked about getting enough for a meal. I mentally added this one to the pot as I pointed the modified barrel at a spot above the rabbit's head, out of habit, and pulled the trigger. The shot was close and I wanted to catch the cottontail's head in the edge of the pattern as I had done on snowshoes countless times. Instead of dying like it was supposed to, the rabbit jumped into high gear going straight away. All the pellets had gone harmlessly over the bunny's head. The running shot was actually an easy one, also, and I managed to get off a second round from my pump gun, but I was so flabbergasted, I missed that one too.

The difference between the way cottontails and snowshoes sit when they stop accounted for the miss at the motionless target. When snowshoes stop—other hares, too—they usually sit upright with their head and ears elevated above their bodies. They present a target hunters can draw a good bead on. By blocking out the head, or even lining up on the ears when the distance is far enough for a pattern to open, you will have a hare in the bag every time, with few, if any, pellets in the meat.

Those cowardly cottontails, on the other hand, flatten themselves on the ground when they stop, keeping their ears laid back and their heads on a level with their bodies. This difference between rabbits and hares is a minor one, but it was enough to save that cottontail's life, making the results significant to me. That's why the lesson made a lasting impression. I quickly adjusted, and other rabbits paid the price.

Countless cottontails are collected by North American hunters every year in much the same way Jim and I hunted—walking side by side 30 to 50 yards apart, through good habitat, always keeping track of one another's position. The same technique also works for hares. Other game, too. In fact, probably as many rabbits and hares are shot this way by hunters actually after pheasants, quail, grouse, and woodcock as those taken by serious rabbit hunters—if not more. The tactic is adaptable for any number of hunters from one to ten.

Jump shooting is a good method for hunters who are specifically interested in rabbits and hares. It works well anyplace. Last winter I joined Fred Bruins and his brother-in-law Jack Burt in southern Ontario on a European hare hunt. The fairly open farmland was broken by parallel fencelines about 100 yards apart. Each of

Fred Bruins walks a fenceline in Ontario looking for European hares to jump.

us would take one fenceline, and walk them parallel to each other. The country was open, and it was possible to see the person next to you.

Once in the field, or as you enter it, load your rifles or shotguns. Be ready—a shot can come at any time. That's something Fred forgot to do at a critical point that morning. He was using a lever-action .22 rifle. When we left the car he put some long rifle bullets in the tube leading to the chamber, but he didn't work the action to lever a shell into the chamber.

In short order, Fred jumped a hare (they call them jack rabbits locally), lined up his sights perfectly, and squeezed the trigger, no doubt contemplating a kill as I had on that squatting cottontail. When nothing happened, he recovered quickly and managed to get off a number of shots; some of them came close, but not close enough.

European hares like to hide along the foundations of old buildings and at the bases of trees and bushes, as well as along fencelines, according to my hosts, and can be jumped from these locations. They will also hide under the snow, digging one or two holes. If you come across a hole or two in the snow in the range of these hares and there are hare tracks present, get ready for action. Fred said he once came across two holes that had been excavated by a hare, and as he bent over, looking into one of the holes, the hare came running out of the other one at 30 miles an hour.

Jump shooting is the way Bud Oakland and his friends hunt black-tailed and white-tailed jacks in Idaho. They use centerfire rifles, and occasionally handguns, for this type of hunting. There are often six riflemen in the party, but he said seven is a better number. Bud explained that if there are only one or two hunters, jacks normally sneak off to the sides or out in front of them unseen.

They hunt sagebrush country and spread out in a line even with one another 30 to 50 yards apart. The hunters stay that way, too, for reasons of safety. The rule is that as soon as the shooting starts, every-

European hare (hanging) bagged in New York is three to four times the size of cottontail lying on snow. (Photo by Joe Dell)

Rob Manes (*left*) and Gene Brehm walk through weedy field in Kansas hoping to jump black-tailed jacks.

one stops. Anyone who violates that rule or gets out of line isn't given a second chance.

When the jacks are plentiful, this technique usually yields lots of shooting. One year Bud made six trips after jacks and went through 6,000 rounds of ammunition, averaging 1,000 rounds per trip. He handloads his own ammo, which makes the expenditure of so much lead cheaper than it would otherwise be. Bullets are purchased in quantities of 10,000 and 50,000 at a time. He said bullet weight in flat shooting calibers doesn't matter.

Bud has put so many rounds through his model 70 .22 swift, he's gone through three barrels. He's also used a .22 hornet, .22/250, .222 and .223, all bolt actions. The experienced rifleman said he doesn't recommend the .22 swift and .22/250; they heat up too fast when there is a lot of action.

When jumped, some jacks run a short distance and then stop, offering sitting targets. Most shots are at running jacks, though, and hitting them with a rifle bullet isn't easy. Overall, Bud said about 60 percent of his shots connect.

It takes experience and guesswork to score on jacks in high gear, according to Oakland. He said it's sometimes possible to see where bullets hit when they kick up dirt, and the lead or hold can be adjusted accordingly. When a hare is running hard broadside about 100 yards away, Bud guessed that he leads them by 5 to 6 feet. The hardest rifle shot, according to him, is an animal going straight away. Most shots at jumped jacks are at a distance of 100–150 yards, but the opportunity for longer ones do occur, like the hare dropped at 255 yards with a .44 magnum handgun, mentioned in chapter 6.

The jacks Bud and his buddies bag are sold for mink food. Some taxidermists also buy these hares to make jackalopes or jackdeer from the capes.

A slightly different twist to jump shooting, possible with woodland species of rabbits and hares, is kicking brush piles. This type of cover is a favorite hiding place for both cottontails and snowshoe hares. Brush piles are common wherever there's been some brush trimming or tree cutting. Piles of boards, logs, and other debris that rabbits and hares can hide under can be considered in the same category.

Dave Raikko kicks at a pile of logs—a perfect hiding place for cottontails. Rabbits are easier to flush out of smaller piles of debris.

Stacks of freshly trimmed brush and tops of recently cut or fallen trees may be attractive to rabbits and hares for food, especially during the winter, as well as shelter. The bark and foliage of evergreen trees may be more nutritious than other food items within reach and will attract bunnies for this reason. In a sense, they can have their cake and eat it, too.

Wherever they are present, piles of brush and trees should be the center of attention. Move from one to the next, either alone or with a partner, kicking, probing, or even stomping on them. You're trying to chase any rabbit or hares that might be under them, out in the open. The safest way to stomp brush piles is with a partner. The guy doing the stomping should be gunless while the partner waits ready for a shot. It is easy to lose your balance and fall while you're up on a brush pile. If this happens with a gun in hand, it will be difficult to control the direction of the muzzle and the firearm could discharge accidentally, with disastrous results.

Jim Muscat told me he once jumped on a brush pile while hunting with a friend; when a rabbit ran out he swung on it, losing his balance as he was about to shoot. The gun, a semiautomatic, fired not once, but twice, as he fell. He had no idea where it was pointed. For a few seconds Jim was gripped with terror, thinking he might have accidentally shot his friend. Fortunately, he didn't.

Old brush piles are worth checking as well as new ones. Even though there's no food present in the pile itself, if edibles are close by the shelter will often suit a rabbit's or hare's fancy. Last winter on a hunt with Uncle George and his son Craig, we broke out into an old clearcut littered with piles of brush bordering a cedar swamp.

Craig Smith retrieves snowshoe jumped from old brushpile in clearcut area.

In the opening, there were numerous saplings, which I knew snowshoes will feed on.

One exceptionally large, thick pile caught my eye, especially when I noted a set of tracks made early that morning disappearing into it. I told Craig to get in a position where he could watch the far side of the jumble of brush and be ready to shoot. Then I moved toward the potential hare hideout from the opposite side. Just before I reached it, Craig shot twice, connecting on a snowshoe that moved out ahead of me.

The best action I've experienced by far on snowshoes when jump shooting is from brush piles of aspen or white cedar that was cut that same fall or winter. Hares love the bark of aspen trees and the foliage of cedars. Trimmed cedar tops also provide plenty of cover.

Jim Haveman kicks pile of tops from aspen and cedar trees, ready for a shot at a hare that may be hiding there.

As an example, Jim Haveman joined me one day during February in snowshoe country. We visited a small spot where both aspen and cedar had been cut the previous fall and tops were piled together. In a span of about 30 minutes we had four hares from that clump of brush. I carried my .22 rifle and Jim his shotgun.

I spotted the first snowshoe before we got to the cover. It was hunkered under-neath one of the piles of tops. The .22 claimed that one. Hare number 2 bolted from the next pile of brush when I kicked it. I took a snapshot as it went away, missing. Then it stopped with a maze of thin branches between us. I tried to pick an opening to shoot through, but the last two rounds in the rifle were deflected. However, the jack sat there while I quickly jammed more shells in. Two or three more rounds were deflected after I reloaded, but the next bullet found an opening and its intended target.

The third brush pile held still another hare. This one took some serious prodding before finally hopping into the open and stopping to see what all the commotion was about. It was in perfect position for Jim, but he told me to take the shot because he was concerned about smearing it at that distance with his open-choked gun. I had to shift positions to shoot and that was enough to start the jack moving again. Jim took the shot, scoring.

There was a dry spell before we disturbed the fourth hare from one of the last brush piles. It showed more concern about our presence than the others, heading away at full tilt. Jim's second shot rolled it.

Cottontails may offer sitting shots after exiting brush piles, but don't count on it. They normally have their after-burners on.

15

Stalking and Still-hunting

One time in Wyoming I decided to see how close I could get to a white-tailed jack I had spotted from a distance of about 50 yards. The hare was in easy rifle range, but I had cameras with me that day, so tried for some closeup photographs.

It was December and there were about six inches of snow on the ground. The habitat was open with a few weeds here and there. The hare was grayish-white in color and was nestled in a depression it had dug in the snow, basically relying on natural camouflage for protection. There was no question the jack saw me, but as long as it didn't feel threatened, I thought it would probably remain where it was.

I advanced a few feet at a time, stopping after each bit of progress to snap a few photos and study the whitetail. All my movements were slow and deliberate, and I eventually managed to creep to within

five feet of that hare. It probably took me at least 30 minutes to get that close. The jack got so accustomed to my presence it left its form and started feeding on nearby weeds, and I got some terrific photos. I wasn't in some park where jacks are protected, either. In fact, this was in view of a major interstate freeway. The jacks were at a high point in their population then, which might have had something to do with the animal's behavior; they don't seem as wary then as when they are scarce. At any rate, my point here is that if I had had archery equipment or a handgun instead of a camera, my stalk would have put me in excellent position for an easy shot at that whitetail.

Two days earlier, the same thing happened with a cottontail, also in Wyoming with a camera. The rabbit was uphill from me on a relatively barren slope with just a

This western cottontail ran by me to get to its burrow entrance and sat there ten yards away when I stalked it with camera in Wyoming.

and East. Perhaps it's because western cottontails aren't hunted as heavily as those in other parts of the country.

Because the terrain in much of the West, plus parts of the Midwest, Canada and Alaska, is so open, a technique unique to those regions can be used. It's called *spotting and stalking*. Rabbits or hares are spotted from a distance with binoculars, spotting scope, or naked eyes, then the hunter stalks closer for a shot. This hunting method is most applicable to hunters using rimfire .22 rifles, handguns, or archery equipment. Those who choose to use scoped centerfire rifles can often try long shots from where rabbits and hares are spotted without having to stalk closer. However, a short stalk may be required by riflemen equipped with iron sights or those who want to limit their shots to 100 yards or less.

A biologist I spoke with in Alaska said it is usually possible to get within 100 yards of that state's tundra hares. Hunters

few scraggly sagebrush bushes. The day was sunny and felt warm after a subzero morning. Apparently the bunny was out to eat and soak up some sun.

I walked slowly toward the rabbit, then stopped and took some photos. Before I could advance farther, it ran, but came toward me instead of away. It went right by me and stopped about 10 yards away. I took some more shots, then tried to close the distance between us. When I moved it ducked down into its burrow, which it had stopped next to. That explained why the rabbit ran toward me. Its burrow was the only means of escape.

Here again, I could have had a pitifully easy bow or handgun shot before the cottontail disappeared. Like jacks, rabbits were also abundant. Nonetheless, I was in a real hunting situation that is common with cottontails in the West. Those rabbits are a different kind of critter, behaviorwise, than their cousins in the Midwest

John Koons (*left*) and Mike Lowin with white-tailed jacks they stalked and shot with .22 rifles. (Photo by Ron Spomer)

use rimfire .22s, .222s or .218s, he said. He added, however, that many of the big hares taken are bagged incidental to other types of hunting or trapping.

In some cases there may be cover present that will hide the hunter from a hare or rabbit's view during part or all of a stalk. Changes in the terrain such as gullies, valleys, hills, and ridges will screen hunters. So will rocks, trees, and bushes. When no cover is present and bowhunters or handgunners want to get as close as possible, try moving in slowly, pausing regularly. Moving at an angle toward the quarry may be better than a direct approach, although advancing straight toward rabbits and hares will sometimes work, as I discovered on that white-tailed jack and cottontail.

On long stalks hunters will temporarily lose sight of hares and rabbits, so it helps to become as familiar as possible with the surroundings near the intended goal. Pick out specific landmarks to key in on once there. If you're hunting with a partner, work out a set of hand signals so you can help direct each other silently.

All stalks won't work out as planned, but that's typical of other hunting techniques, too. No method always works. The more you try, the more your rate of success should improve. Hunters who try to move in too fast are more apt to fail than those who are patient enough to pause for minutes at a time and advance slowly when they do move, especially when in sight of jacks and rabbits.

In situations where cottontails are stationed on the edges of their burrows when a shot is taken, gun hunters should try for head shots and clean kills. Bowhunters can try for head shots, too, but chest hits with blunts should have the desired effect. Even when killed instantly, some rabbits will slide into their burrows. If the dead animal can't be reached by hand, try retrieving the carcass with a length of barbed wire. Extend the wire into the hole until you make contact with the rabbit, then twist it, working to tangle the fur in the barbs. A broadhead-tipped arrow may work to skewer an underground carcass and raise it to the surface, too. One more tool that can extend a hunter's reach 8 to 10 inches is a hemostat. These elongated forceps lock in a closed position, reducing the chances of dropping a rabbit held in their grasp.

In brushland and wooded terrain, spotting and stalking rabbits and hares often aren't possible. In these situations hunters should use a similar technique: *still-hunting*. Once potential hunting grounds are located—based on sign, habitat preferences of the rabbit or hare you are after, and perhaps actual sightings—the idea is to sneak through the cover slowly, trying to spot rabbits and hares before they spot you. As with snow tracking, the object is to use your eyes more than your feet; you should spend more time standing still than walking. When you do move ahead, move slowly and stealthily, sneaking forward just far enough to get a different vantage point on bushes, trees, and clumps of cover that are potential hiding spots for hares and rabbits. Look them all over carefully before proceeding farther.

When they're sitting tight, hares will crouch down and lay their ears back along their backs the same way cottontails do, so you're looking for an animal that is actually only a fraction of the size it would be when sitting up or running. Their backs will only be a few inches above the ground. Keep your eyes peeled for out-of-place horizontal lines—they might be a

When hiding, snowshoe hares will hunker down like rabbits, so when you're still-hunting, look close to ground level. Note how this hare's eye and white ear stand out.

rabbit or hare's back. Fallen and decaying trees will account for some horizontal lines in their otherwise vertical-oriented surroundings, but not all. Off-color or distinctive parts of anatomy such as eyeballs and ears may tip you off to the presence of a rabbit or hare, too.

Some of the most enjoyable and productive still-hunts I have taken part in have been for hares when their natural camouflage backfires. Sometimes they turn white during late fall or early winter before snow covers the ground. Or sometimes the snow that helped hide them melts, making them easier to spot. In many cases, they stand out like a sore thumb.

Most of my still-hunts for white hares in contrasting surroundings have involved snowshoes, but the same principle would apply to white-tailed jacks, Arctic, and

Dan White got close to this cottontail by still-hunting.

Snowshoe hares that turn white when there's no snow will sit tight for bowhunter and those carrying handguns. At times like these, their "camouflage" coloration works against them and for the hunter.

tundra hares, all of which change coat color. None of these hares have control over when they turn from brown or gray to white. And it doesn't happen automatically after the first snowfall. The molt is a gradual process that is triggered by changing daylength (photoperiod) in the fall and in spring. Hares actually complete their coat color changes at approximately the same time every year. Their feet and ears commonly become white first, followed by body fur.

At times when hares contrast with their surroundings, they are instinctively aware of their vulnerability. So they hide as best as they can and are reluctant to move, unless they absolutely have to. When jacks sit so tight, hunters can often approach them extremely close. These circumstances are particularly ideal for bowhunters and handgunners.

If you are lucky enough to time a hunt when hares are most visible, you no longer have to worry about spotting a tiny eye. Look for the whole animal. Any spot of white that you see should be investigated.

Birch bark will result in some false alarms, but some of the patches of white will be hares, if you're looking in the right spots. Hares will do their best to keep as much of their easy-to-see hides out of sight as possible, remaining in the thickest cover available. Look in hollow logs and stumps and under brush piles, where jacks can totally vanish from sight.

Even though snowshoes are easy to see and sit tight when their camouflage backfires, collecting them with a bow or handgun isn't always a cinch. The thick cover snowshoes often hide in makes scoring with both a handgun and arrows a challenge even though they cooperate by sitting still. I found this out the first time I tried hunting hares with a handgun.

It was mid-November in Michigan and gun deer season was open. I had tagged a white-tailed buck (the antlered kind) soon after the season opened, but my partners hadn't, so I strapped on a .22 revolver. While handgunning for hares there was a chance I might move some deer past my partners. Spooky white-tailed deer are

Mark Eby takes aim at hare that thinks it's hidden.

spooking the hare, I slowly eased my revolver out of its holster, thumbed the hammer back as I raised it, and took careful aim.

I expected the critter to crumple at the shot, but it just sat there. The same thing happened on the next three shots, and I began wondering if there was something wrong with my shells or the gun. However, the fifth shot connected. Those first four bullets were deflected by brush and never made it through to the hare despite my best efforts at aiming for small openings.

Getting an arrow through to that first hare probably would have been even tougher than a .22 bullet. Although that one remained stationary long enough for me to connect, they don't always do that, as I soon found out on the second one spotted that day. It gave me one shot with my handgun, which missed, then hightailed it for parts unknown.

Once white snowshoes start moving on bare ground they sometimes keep going until they find another sanctuary far removed from what disturbed them. But they will occasionally stop once or twice after they leave their form, before heading out in high gear.

I didn't spot hare number 3, for example, until it hopped into the open. The snowshoe was hiding in cover that obscured it from view. When I was within a matter of feet of its hiding place, it zipped out in front of me and stopped. The bunny held still long enough for me to make good on the opportunity.

A third jack was added to my game pouch later in the day. It was hiding under an evergreen tree, and it took three .22 slugs before one found a path through the branches and needles to reach the hare.

Still-hunting alone is fine, but this technique can also be enjoyed with a partner

attracted to the same thick, swampy lowland cover that appeals to snowshoe hares hoping to stay out of sight.

I worked my way through a tag alder swale filled with high marsh grass, looking carefully for patches of white that might prove to be hiding hares. Before long I spotted what I was looking for—a snowshoe hunkered under an umbrella of grass with alder branches screening it from the side. I was close, probably about 15 yards away. To reduce the chances of or two. You can still-hunt parallel to one another, hoping that hares that get away from one person may be bagged by a buddy, or each can go off in different directions to compare notes later. I prefer the parallel approach.

Mark Eby and I were hunting in early December; I carried a bow and Mark had a handgun. We spent a morning in a thick stand of young spruce trees bordered by brushy cover that was littered with fallen

White snowshoe I bagged while still-hunting in thick spruce.

trees and hollow stumps. There was enough cover to hide hundreds of hares in that location. We positioned ourselves about 50 yards apart and snuck along, trying our best to spot hiding hares.

Before long we spotted not one but two snowshoes at about the same time, approximately 50 yards apart. Mark had a good shot at one that was huddled just inside a hollow log, and collected it quickly. I had to change positions to get a clear shot at the second jack, and it ran as I did. I whistled in an effort to stop the fleeing bunny, but it kept going.

A sudden, sharp noise like a whistle will sometimes stop an alerted rabbit or hare in its tracks if it isn't spooked too badly. The animals apparently can't hear as well while running as they can while sitting, and they stop in an effort to determine the source of the sound. A rabbit or hare that has already determined it might be in danger, like the one I whistled at, is less likely to respond favorably than one that hasn't seen you.

Minutes after I missed my opportunity for a shot, I got another chance at a hare under a fallen tree. The odds of getting an arrow through the branches didn't look good, but I surprised myself by making the shot count.

I didn't spot the next snowshoe hiding under a thick spruce tree until I was less than 10 yards away. It was an easy shot. That gave me two and Mark one, but he got a chance to even the score before the morning was over.

The spruces hid two more hares ahead of us. The first one was a bit jumpy and vacated the premises when Mark tried to maneuver for a shot. The second was comfortable enough where it was to remain in place, even after Mark missed a shot. Its luck ran out on shot number 2.

We saw five more snowshoes during an evening hunt, and collected two of those. Our tally for the day was eleven hares seen and six bagged, which is respectable in anyone's book considering we were hunting with a handgun and bow. An average rate of success for this type of hunting, based on my experience, is 50 percent, and that's about what we came up with.

Cottontails can be still-hunted in the snow when they contrast with their surroundings as easily as white hares without snow. Western cottontails are sure to be more cooperative than those in the eastern half of the continent because they aren't as jumpy. When rabbit populations are at a low point, though, they can be tough to come by wherever they live.

16

Take a Stand

Bruce Dupras waited patiently in a tree stand on the edge of a swamp for game to show. He was bowhunting and had his compound bow, an arrow on the string, hanging within easy reach. It was evening in late October.

As light was beginning to fade, a brown form finally appeared and made its way to apples sprinkled on the ground near Dupras' stand. Bruce grabbed his bow as the animal fed, silently bringing it into position to draw. In a minute or two he was ready for the shot and came to full draw. Just then the game animal looked up and Bruce centered his sight on its chest.

It was over in a split second. My brother-in-law claimed his first bow-killed snowshoe hare. From his stand that fall he had released five arrows at hares. There were three misses, a fourth arrow grazed

its target, and he finally connected on number 5.

All his shots came late in the day, but that's when he did most of his stand hunting. Occasionally a hare saw him move as he maneuvered his bow into position for a shot or brought the arrow back to his anchor point. The alerted snowshoes usually bolted, but as long as Bruce kept still, they went only a short distance before stopping and eventually returning to feed.

Bruce wasn't actually hunting hares. He was stand hunting for white-tailed deer. Baiting for deer is legal in Michigan and is a common technique used by bowhunters to try to get shots at deer. Besides the deer, local snowshoes took a liking to the apples. So the hares provided an added bonus to his deer hunting, in the same way rabbits and hares are often bonus game to upland bird hunters.

Portable tree stands like this one made by Baker are good for getting shots at hares, and sometimes rabbits, at feeding areas. Stand hunting has for the most part been ignored as a rabbit and hare hunting tactic, but it works.

My brother-in-law's experience isn't an isolated case either. Bob Wood also reported getting and taking shots at snowshoes while bowhunting for deer from a stand. Although he saw most hares in the evening, he recalls some sightings early in the morning, too. Bowhunter Dave Bigelow nailed a snowshoe from a tree stand one November morning when it hopped up on a log at a distance of 36 yards. Dave is an excellent shot. Most bow shots at rabbits and hares are at 25 yards or less.

Mike Pollard has arrowed five or six snowshoes from a stand while bowhunting for deer; in fact, he could have shot many others that he simply watched rather than take a chance at spooking an incoming deer. He knows of other bowhunters who have done the same thing.

I've seen snowshoes while stand hunting for deer, too. Lots of them. There's a difference between my experience and those of the others, though. In most cases, I wasn't hunting over bait, but simply posted along deer trails or watching buck scrapes during the rut. One fall I hunted South Fox Island in Lake Michigan, with a high hare population. I saw them every morning and evening wherever I sat. Other hunters did, too.

One memorable evening I saw three hares. I don't know if I could have gotten them all with my bow, but I certainly would have with a .22 rifle. What sticks in my mind about that particular evening wasn't the number of hares I saw—I have seen more than that on other occasions—but what one of them did.

The third hare came along late in the day. It hopped toward me, and I sat perfectly still on a seat with my feet on the ground. That hare kept coming until it was right at my feet, then proceeded to chew on my leather boots! No kidding! I could feel its teeth gnawing on the boot through the layer of leather. The strength of the hare's jaws was readily apparent. An accumulation of salt on the leather from a perspiring foot is probably what was so appealing to the jack. At any rate, I sat there rigid as a rock for a few minutes with my eyes staring straight ahead, figuring if I moved my head to look down the snowshoe would run off. There was a good chance I could have caught that hare by hand, or at least scared it to death trying, but I was too amazed by what was happening. When I had enough of the bunny's chewing, I simply moved my foot and it hopped off.

Whenever rabbit or hare numbers are high I don't think they are as cautious as they would otherwise be. The animals also seem to be more active, increasing the chances of being seen by a stationary hunter.

Another time that I saw snowshoes when stand hunting, food was involved, but it was a natural supply created by logging, not bait I had put there. White cedar had been cut and the hares were coming in to nibble on the nutritious tops. I saw two hares that December evening.

Cottontails can also be taken from a stand, but they are much tougher to get a shot at than hares, at least with a bow. Long-time bowhunter George Gardner said he may have had about 100 opportunities at cottontails from tree stands over the years and has gotten only 2 of them.

He said the problem is it is difficult to get a shot off at a rabbit because they are so alert for danger from above by hawks and owls, that the slightest movement sends them scurrying into cover. Lifting just one finger has been enough to spook cottontails in position for a bow shot, according to Gardner.

A hunter who is well concealed, either in an elevated stand or on the ground, is less likely to be seen by a rabbit, of course. And due to the spooky nature of cottontails, at least in the eastern half of their range, a shotgun would up the odds in the stand hunter's favor over a bow and arrow. The scattergun would allow a shot in situations when rabbits started running, which would be often, according to Gardner's experience.

I point all this out to present a case for hunting rabbits and hares from a stand. It is possible. It has been done, usually inci-

dental to deer hunting. But it has been virtually ignored as a hunting technique specifically for these small game animals. I've been aware of the possibilities myself for a number of years and have planned on doing it, knowing it would work, but thus far haven't followed through on my intentions. That will change.

I know of only one person who has actually hunted hares or rabbits from a stand. It was a young hunter with one year of deer-hunting experience under his belt. He hunted deer from a stand and perhaps saw a snowshoe while so involved, but when he wanted to try specifically for hares during winter, the technique carried over.

The boy either cut aspen and cedar branches to attract hungry hares and built a blind nearby, or built a blind overlooking a food supply that was already there. I really can't remember which. I heard the story about ten years ago. It doesn't really matter anyway; the circumstances were the same either way.

Hares soon started feeding on the preferred food items and the boy hunted religiously from his stand morning and evening with bow and arrow. He eventually bagged two bunnies and missed other shots. To that youngster, success on snowshoes from his blind was probably as exciting and stimulating as deer hunting. The experience no doubt helped when it came to future deer hunts, too.

As a matter of fact, hunting techniques covered in three of the four previous chapters, as well as this one, can also be applied to deer hunting. These tactics are actually the most popular ones for connecting on white-tailed deer. Jump shooting is the only method that applies primarily to rabbits and hares. Hunters who become good at tracking, driving, stalking, still-hunting, and stand hunting for rabbits and hares are bound to benefit from the experience when they apply it to deer hunting.

These types of small game hunting are good practice for deer hunting, for adults as well as youngsters. The opposite can also be true, as the example about the boy who did hunt hares from a stand illustrates. So why haven't more hunters tried to hunt rabbits and hares from a stand?

Many of them haven't thought of it, or they use other methods that produce satisfactory results. Bob Wood and Mike Pollard are avid hare hunters, for example,

but they both have beagles. When they plan a hunt, it revolves around their hounds, and that's only natural.

Bob mentioned another consideration. He hunts deer from a stand and doesn't normally get serious about trying for snowshoes until after deer season is over. By the time his deer hunt ends, he's had his fill of sitting in a stand. Many of the hours spent waiting for a deer are uneventful, if not downright boring, because no game is in sight. So he's ready to move around and see some action once he starts chasing rabbits. Even if Bob didn't own beagles, he would probably choose to

A stand overlooking spot like this should prove productive. Hares have been nibbling on the bark of the fallen aspen tree.

do his hare hunting by jump shooting, drives, or tracking.

My preference for tracking, still-hunting, jump shooting, and drives, and for hunting with hounds, has kept me from getting serious about stand hunting until now. I'm convinced enough about the applicability of posting to rabbit and hare hunting that I thought it was worth covering in this book. I'm suggesting it as an alternative for the lone hunter who doesn't have a dog and may be unsure of himself as a tracker and still-hunter, or is simply looking for a "different" way to hunt. Stand hunting may be the most practical technique for the hunter who has a handicap that prohibits him from taking part in hunts employing more active approaches.

As already mentioned, feeding sites are good locations for stands. My preference would be for locations already being used by bunnies, such as downed aspen or cedar trees for snowshoes. Cottontails might be venturing into agricultural fields or apple orchards, or browsing on a clump of saplings. Farm fields and haystacks might attract jacks. An accumulation of sign—droppings, tracks, clipped vegetation, and gnawed bark—plus actual sightings of animals, will be evidence of feeding areas.

If baiting is legal where you hunt, preferred food items can be placed in strategic locations for later stand hunting. Apples and commercial rabbit food can be used as bait. Uncle George put some commercial rabbit pellets around his deer stand last fall and had a snowshoe hare feeding on them within a day during shooting hours. Or use the animals' natural food. Branches can be cut if there aren't any already present on the ground. Trimming a few branches from trees here

and there won't do any harm to trees, but a large-scale thinning may. Cutting trees, unless they belong to you, is not permissible.

When choosing a spot to put bait it is always best to put it either on the edge of heavy cover used by rabbits and hares or in an opening surrounded by security cover. The animals are sure to find the bait quicker when it's positioned in this fashion and are most likely to appear during hours of daylight.

Once you've decided on a place to hunt, you must select the spot where you will wait. Hunting can be done either from the ground or an elevated platform, where legal. Most states and provinces allow bowhunters to operate from tree stands, but it is illegal for gun hunters in some places such as Michigan. If I were to hunt from the ground, I would use natural cover as much as possible, if not entirely, to screen me from a rabbit or hare's view and to avoid altering the site. However, satisfactory blinds can be erected without much time, effort, or disturbance.

Portable climbing tree stands like those made by Baker are handy for this type of hunting. They are quick and easy to put up and take down. Branches should be used to break an elevated hunter's outline as much as possible. When hunting from a tree stand I try to situate myself on the opposite side of the tree trunk from where I expect game to appear. This way, the trunk provides concealment even if no branches are present.

I never consider wind direction when hunting rabbits and hares because I've never seen evidence that they use their noses to detect danger. The hare that chewed on my boot obviously didn't use its nose to identify my presence. However, hunters in stands would be in a better

Also worth a try are stands overlooking snowshoe hare trails like this, especially where two or more intersect.

position to determine if wind direction makes a difference in success and can move accordingly, if it does.

Although stand hunting at feeding sites is usually a good choice, there are other possibilities. A post overlooking two or more heavily used trails can produce results, as can a spot overlooking a thick patch of cover where rabbits and hares spend much of the day. Watching bedding areas increases the chances of seeing bunnies as early as possible in the evening; they might not return to these areas until after daylight in the morning.

Snowshoe hares do enough roaming that it's possible to see them using trails, and the same is true for cottontails. Biologist Kenneth Sadler with the Missouri Department of Conservation said cottontails may feed in one location for a while when they first leave their forms in the evening, but then they move around, doing a lot of sampling of various food items they encounter.

Early and late in the day are obviously the best times to see rabbits and hares from a stand because those are when they are most active. This may not be as true during cold winter days, though, at least for cottontails. Rabbits should be most active during the warmest time of the day, which might be at midday, but could coincide with the evening. Bud Oakland in Idaho said shooting jacks that are raiding haystacks is possible at night while using a light, but a permit must be obtained from the Department of Fish and Game first.

Despite the fact that true stand hunting has been virtually ignored as a tactic for taking rabbits and hares, a form of the technique has been employed by white-tailed jack hunters in South Dakota and probably in other locations with similar habitat. Fellow writer and photographer Ron Spomer informed me about it. He said that when deep snow conditions exist, whitetails concentrate in shelter belts. On windy days with blowing snow, these shelter belts provide the best protection from the elements.

Ron said the hares will move out ahead of a hunter as he walks through a shelter belt, providing some tricky shooting. Much better shots will be possible if he holds his fire and picks a spot to sit and wait. The whitetails often start filtering back into the cover in about 15 minutes, according to Spomer, sometimes hopping within close range, but always providing better targets than when jumped initially.

This same technique will also work on snowshoe hares, sometimes. Some hares have favorite forms, and if jumped from them will return, if given the chance. Snowshoes that only go a short distance without any further disturbance may soon return. Hares that are pushed or go a long way when jumped, may wait until evening to return.

17

Care of Carcasses

Rabbits and hares are the easiest game animals to skin and dress, in my estimation. There are at least a couple of ways to do it, and in one of them—the quickest and the easiest—it isn't even necessary to remove the entrails. The step-by-step process is demonstrated on a cottontail by Wayne Van Zwoll in Kansas. (See photos.)

The vast majority of the edible meat on a rabbit or hare carcass can be removed in this manner without having to handle the viscera. The only salvageable part that is discarded is the rib cage and neck. Since I often cook the rib cages for my dog, and sometimes the front legs, too, I normally take a few more minutes to dress carcasses.

Another sequence of photos shows George Smith skinning, dressing, and butchering a snowshoe hare. Since the skin peels easily from rabbit and hare car-

casses, especially soon after they are bagged, there are a number of ways to start the skinning process. A knife isn't necessary to break the skin.

The hind legs are a good place to start the skinning process. While holding the hind feet firmly in one hand, grip a fold of skin with the other hand and pull forward or downward, depending on how the rabbit or hare is positioned. The skin pulls away from the carcass without much effort. I normally start pulling skin free at the tendons that connect to the rear of hind feet, but it's possible to start anywhere.

After a fold of skin is pulled free from the hind legs, continue working your way forward until the skin is removed from the entire carcass, except for head and feet. In some cases, the skin can be removed in one large piece. If it rips, it will have to

Wayne Van Zwoll demonstrates the quickest and easiest method of skinning and dressing (*1*). The animal must be skinned first. Pull a fold of skin upward on the center of the back. Insert knife blade through the skin and cut upward, separating the skin on the back (*left*). (*2*) Then grip the skin on each side of the cut and pull the skin off the carcass, half in each direction (*right*).

(*3*) The skin easily peels away from the meat in two major pieces.

(*4*) This is what the carcass should look like when skinned.

(*5*) Break leg bones at ankles.

(*6*) Then use a knife to remove feet from the carcass. If you have a hatchet or meat cleaver handy, they work better.

(7) Remove front legs and shoulders from carcass by cutting connective tissue.

(8) Cut hind legs free from the carcass where they join the body at hip joints. It doesn't matter in what order legs are removed. Some hunters cut away hind legs before front shoulders.

(9) The final step is removal of loins from either side of the backbone on the top of the back. Make cuts as deep as possible next to the backbone.

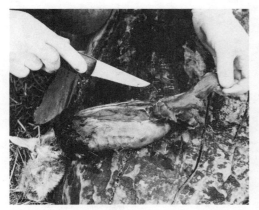

(10) Then separate these boneless pieces of meat from the back by grasping one end of the loin and lifting it as it is sliced away from the carcass with the knife. Once the loins are removed, the ungutted carcass can be discarded.

(11) End results: six pieces of meat that can be cleaned and prepared for a meal, or packaged and frozen for later use.

George Smith demonstrates the skinning, dressing, and butchering process. (*1*) A knife isn't required to break the skin of rabbits and hares for skinning. The thin skin tears easily when a fold is gripped firmly and pulled away from the body. I always start skinning from the hind legs and work forward, as George does here.

come in several chunks. Either way, the process can usually be accomplished quickly and without much difficulty.

When you reach the front legs, it sometimes helps to free the skin from them by bending them at the joint and pushing them upward while pulling the skin downward around them with the other hand.

Once a rabbit or hare carcass is skinned, the entrails can be removed. Use the point of a knife blade to cut the thin muscle covering the lower body cavity from the base of the ribs to a point between the hind legs. The cut can also be started between the legs. Wherever you begin, take care not to cut too deeply, rupturing intestines or stomach. The lower body cavity wall is usually thin enough that viscera can be seen through it, which reduces the chances of cutting too deeply.

Innards can be pulled out easily and discarded after the body cavity is open. Remove the contents of the abdominal cavity first, which includes the intestines,

(*2*) The skin pulls away from the carcass in one large piece in many cases, especially when the animal is still warm.

(3) If the skin doesn't invert over front legs, bend them at the joint and push them upward while pulling hide down around them.

stomach, liver, and kidneys. The liver is dark red and is located toward the front of the abdominal cavity near the stomach and diaphragm (a thin muscle that separates the chest cavity from the abdominal cavity).

If you're concerned about tularemia, examine the liver for swelling and the presence of tiny white spots. Refer to the chapter on tularemia for a photo of the liver of an infected animal, and for an explanation of other white marks that may be seen on the liver that are not a sign of tularemia. If you're interested in what rabbits or hares were eating, their stomachs can be opened and the contents examined.

To get at the heart and lungs, pull out the diaphragm. The heart and lungs can be pulled out together if you grasp them and the windpipe together, and break the windpipe. It is easier to reach and remove

(4) Use the point of a knife blade to open the carcass to remove entrails. Be careful not to cut too deep.

(5) Remove the contents of the abdominal cavity first, once cut is complete. The intestines, stomach, and liver will practically fall out.

(6) Discard viscera in a hole in the snow or cover with dirt.

(7) Remove contents of the chest cavity next, primarily the heart and lungs, by reaching up to front of chest cavity and gripping windpipe with organs.

(8) Heart and lungs are extracted.

(9) **Head can be twisted loose by gripping it as shown.**

(10) **Once neck is broken, use a knife to cut muscle tissue, or simply pull the head off.**

heart and lungs if you extend the opening in the abdominal cavity through the ribs, although this is not necessary.

Turn your attention to the anal area after contents of the chest cavity are removed. Cut away loose skin under the tail that extends behind rear legs, if present, then push a finger or small knife blade through the pelvic area from the inside of the body cavity to remove any droppings and any pieces of the lower digestive tract that may remain.

As final steps in the dressing process, the feet and head can be removed. The head can be twisted free from the carcass by gripping the front quarters of the carcass firmly in one hand and the head in

the opposite hand as shown. Then twist the head until the neck breaks free. A hatchet or cleaver, if one is handy, makes this step easier.

Take care to dispose of entrails properly, especially if you're dressing rabbits or hares in the field and dogs are present. Tapeworm cysts are frequently in viscera from rabbits and hares and they will infect dogs if ingested. I often field dress bunnies I've bagged before leaving an area, having first put the dogs safely in the vehicle. Nonetheless, it's still a good idea to bury entrails.

If there's snow on the ground it's a simple matter to kick a hole in the snow, then cover it once done dressing the day's bag.

On bare ground, a shovel can be used to dig a hole to bury viscera. Alternatives are to dispose of innards in depressions under rocks or logs or to hang them in trees or brush where they will dry out.

One thing rabbit and hare hunters should refrain from doing is field dressing their game right next to roads, leaving blood and guts for others to see. This is unsightly to anyone, but especially non-hunters, and only serves to hurt the image of hunters. The remains of rabbits left on the ground are usually cleaned up quickly by scavengers, but there is no excuse for leaving them where they may be visible to other people.

I do a lot of rabbit and hare hunting during the winter when there's snow on the ground and frequently use the white stuff to wipe out excess blood from field dressed carcasses and then to clean my hands. When there isn't any snow present, dried grass, leaves, or paper towels can be used to wipe carcasses. One advantage of wearing surgical gloves when dressing rabbits, besides escaping the chances of infection from tularemia, is that your hands don't get bloody. Blood comes off with the gloves.

Excess blood in carcasses will drain away if they are hung in an upright position for a short period of time. It may be beneficial to leave heads on carcasses that will be hung until after they are drained. Heads can usually be wedged between limbs and tree trunks for easy hanging.

If the intestines or the stomach has been ruptured, either when the animal was shot or during dressing, wipe away as much of the loose material as possible. Cut away any pieces of meat that become soiled and discard them.

Once cleaned, carcasses can be cut into pieces as described earlier, with a couple of minor differences. Both front and hind legs are removed the same way, then the back is separated from the rib section at the base of the ribs. Break the backbone first by bending the carcass at the appropriate spot, and use a knife to separate tissue at the break.

When skinning and dressing bunnies in the field, be sure to bring a plastic bag for the cleaned carcasses. Garbage bags and large food-storage bags will work. If the weather is warm, transport cleaned rabbits *on top of* plastic bags, where air can circulate around them, both in game pouches and in vehicles. Carcasses can be put into bags with no problem in weather that is cool to cold.

To ensure the best quality, it is important that pieces of meat be chilled as quickly as possible when the weather is warm. Bringing a cooler or ice chest along on hunts is a good idea, and carcasses can be put in plastic bags if a cooler is used. If this isn't possible, cuts of meat should be refrigerated as soon as you get home.

Also, in warm weather it may be desirable to field dress rabbits and hares soon after they are bagged to aid in cooling the carcasses. Some hunters prefer doing this regardless of the weather and leave the hide on to keep the carcass clean, doing the skinning at the end of the day.

To simply field dress and not skin a rabbit or hare, grip a hunk of hide on the belly while holding the animal by the hind legs and pull downward, exposing as much area as desired. Opening the chest cavity as well as the abdominal cavity is advisable in warm weather to speed up cooling. Remove the entrails as described earlier.

When skinning and dressing rabbits at home, I try to do it outside when the weather permits, to reduce the chances of getting loose fur in the kitchen or basement. On the days I handle game inside I work over a large paper bag or plastic garbage bag on opened newspaper. The newspaper catches most of the stray fur and blood that doesn't end up in the bag; it gets folded over and discarded after I'm done.

Try to keep cuts of rabbit meat as clean as possible when skinning and dressing the animals. Once at home, they can be rinsed with cold water, removing any bits of hair, blood, or vegetation that may be clinging to them. If the rabbits or hares were bagged with a shotgun, an effort should be made to remove as many pellets as possible that may still be in the meat. Unexpectedly biting down on a piece of lead is a surprise most diners can do without. Loose chips of bone should also be removed.

Shot pellets may be covered with fur that they picked up when entering the animal. Cut into meat along shot channels to remove lead and hair. Areas that contain clotted blood may be sites where BBs are lodged. Pellets that aren't visible can sometimes be felt by squeezing and rubbing pieces of meat between fingers.

Once pieces of meat are totally clean, they can be wrapped and placed in a refrigerator, if they will be used in one to three days. Otherwise, butchered rabbits and hares should be stored in a freezer until ready to use.

Lightweight aluminum foil, food storage bags, and other types of wraps are suitable for storing meat in a refrigerator for short periods of time. I use heavy-duty aluminum foil to wrap rabbit and hare meat for the freezer. The foil is wrapped tightly around the meat to eliminate air, then a piece of masking tape is labeled with information about contents and the

Six pieces from snowshoe hare that was skinned, dressed, and cut into pieces. I often boil the rib cage (*top*), then feed it to my dog. The remainder can be used in meals for the family.

date. Freezer paper can be used to store meat from these game animals, too. Double wrapping can help protect from freezer burn. For best eating, rabbits and hares should be eaten within a year; however, I've had them frozen longer and still had respectable results.

Rabbits and hares that hunters might want to have mounted should be handled differently than those for the table. They should not be skinned or dressed. Since the skins of these game animals are so thin and delicate, skinning should be left up to the taxidermist. If at all possible, take at least one color photograph of the animal when it's fresh so both you and the taxidermist will have a record of what it looked like. Better yet, take a number of photos from different angles.

If there is blood on the carcass, do your best to wipe it off with tissue, paper towels, leaves, or grass when it's fresh. It will be easier to eliminate blood when it's wet than after it dries.

It's best not to put the animal in a game bag, pouch, or vest where hair often gets matted and bent and may be stained with blood. Instead, the carcass should be carried by hand, put somewhere in the field where it will be safe to pick up later, or placed in a vehicle right away. Get the animal to a taxidermist as soon as possible, preferably the same day. If the weather is cold, the animal can be kept in a shed, garage, or other unheated outbuilding until it can be taken to a taxidermist. To store in a freezer, wrap the rabbit or hare loosely in a plastic garbage bag and lay the animal flat. Avoid bending the ears to prevent damage to them.

18

Eating Rabbits and Hares

Some fine eating can be the end result of successful hunts for all types of rabbits and hares, from cottontails to jack rabbits. Most hunters accept the fact that the various species of rabbits are great table fare, along with snowshoe hares, Arctic hares, and European hares. But for some reason, there is a strange prejudice against eating jacks among some hunters. Perhaps it is the fact that in many states where jacks are most abundant, they are considered pests and vermin and little else.

Fortunately, there isn't total bias against eating jacks. Hunters who have eaten these hares aren't shy about saying how good they are.

Myths have a way of perpetuating themselves among hunters without being questioned. One hunter tells another jack rabbits aren't fit to eat and he will probably accept it as gospel without trying

them himself. Before you know it, a large number of hunters are claiming the same thing without one of them having cooked and eaten a jack rabbit. If someone tells you jack rabbits aren't good to eat, ask them how many he's eaten.

Another myth I've heard about snowshoe hares is they are unfit to eat during March and April. This is simply not true. Meat from snowshoes bagged during these months—as well as December, January, and February—has graced my table, and I find little difference in the palatability from one month to the next.

Rabbit and hare hunters can rest assured that whatever they bag will be suitable for the table, provided the carcasses are properly cleaned and cared for, as outlined in the previous chapter. Proper cooking can also make a difference, and that's where this chapter comes in. Following is a sample of some of the recipes that can be used to prepare rabbits and hares for the table. Additional recipes can be found in books devoted entirely to cooking wild game.

Although a particular recipe may be recommended for a specific species of rabbit or hare, they can all be used for any species. My wife Lucy is responsible for some of the recipes we use for rabbits and hares, but we've also borrowed some from friends. We use a lot of cream soups and gravies in our cooking and most often prepare meals that are quick and easy.

Some hunters soak rabbit or hare meat in refrigerated salt water overnight, the evening before it is prepared. I prefer to eliminate this step. The meat can be handled either way.

Manes' Cubed Jack

Cut jack rabbit meat into bite-size pieces. Cover with pancake batter and deep fry.

Trombley's Rabbit Stroganoff

Cut the meat from two or three snowshoe hares into bite-size pieces. Cover pieces with salted flour and brown. Add dry onion soup mix, enough water to cover the meat, and a little Worcestershire sauce. Simmer for about an hour, then add one or two cans of cream of mushroom soup, depending on the consistency desired. The final step is to mix in an 8-ounce container of sour cream. Serve over hot cooked noodles.

Pieces from two snowshoe hares in roasting pan with vegetables for Baked Hare.

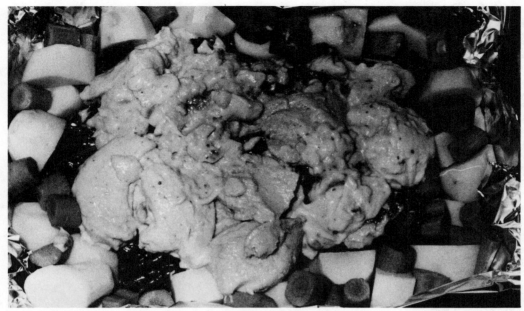

Cream soups have been poured over pieces of hare, then the foil closed and put in the oven for 1½–2 hours at 350 degrees F.

Smith's Strog

Brown pieces of meat without flour coating. Cook for about an hour in two or three cans of chicken broth or gravy. Add sour cream. Serve hot over noodles.

We make a similar meal using soup, which is baked in a casserole dish. Brown cut pieces of meat as before, then add to a casserole dish with one can each of cream of chicken and cream of celery soups. Bake for 1½ hours at 350°F. and serve over noodles.

Andrea's Rabbit Stew

Put legs and backs from two or three rabbits in a kettle of water and cook at a slow boil until the meat separates from bones. Remove bones. Add two medium-size onions, chopped; two stalks of celery, chopped; two medium-size potatoes and four carrots, both diced; and a small can of peas.

Simmer slowly for an hour, then add 2 teaspoons salt, ½ teaspoon pepper, 1 teaspoon each of seasoning salt and sweet basil, and a garlic clove. Simmer for 15 minutes, then stir in 2 tablespoons of cornstarch mixed in ½ cup of cold water. Another 15 minutes, and the stew is ready to serve with hot biscuits.

Fred's Steamed European Hare

Brown cuts from one hare in butter. Add water to pan to cover the bottom, and add sliced onions to suit taste. Put lid on pan and simmer for two hours or until tender.

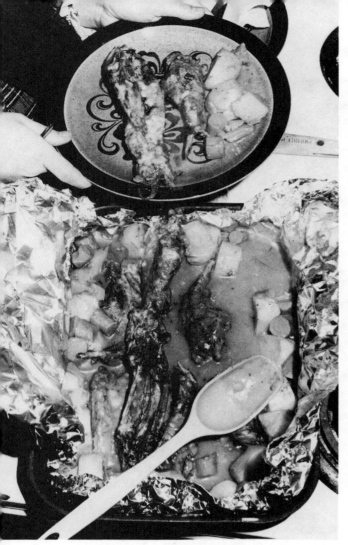

Roast hare, ready to eat.

Baked Hare

Place legs and backs from two hares in a casserole dish and add two cans of cream of mushroom soup. Bake for 1½–2 hours at 350°F. or 1–1½ hours at 375°. The soup makes good gravy for mashed potatoes.

Another method is to cover the bottom of a roasting pan with aluminum foil. Put pieces of rabbit or hare in the foil with cut potatoes, carrots, and onions. Pour your choice of cream soups (chicken, celery, or mushroom) over meat and vegetables, and bake as above.

Van Zwoll's Deep Dish Rabbit Pie

Cook cuts from two rabbits in salt water at a low boil for 1½–2 hours, remove meat from bones, and cut meat into small pieces. Make a sauce from 1 cup of broth rabbit was in, 2 tablespoons flour, and a pinch of salt and pepper. Make stuffing from 3 cups of mashed potatoes or rice, cubes from 8 slices of dry bread, ½ cup celery, 1 tablespoon parsley, 1 teaspoon salt, ½ teaspoon pepper, ½ teaspoon poultry seasoning, 1 well-beaten egg, 1 minced onion, and 2 tablespoons melted butter or margarine.

Put the stuffing and meat in alternate layers in a greased casserole dish until full, sprinkling 2 tablespoons sauce over each layer of meat. Bake at 350°F. for about 30 minutes.

Kansas Noodle Casserole

Parboil rabbit in salt water until meat separates from bones, then cut meat into small pieces. Mix 1 cup grated cheese and 2 cups cooked egg noodles with 1 tablespoon margarine or butter; place in bottom of a greased casserole dish. Put meat on top with 1 can of mushrooms, a pinch of oregano, and 1 teaspoon seasoned salt. Cut tomatoes from a large can into pieces, then pour tomato pieces and juice on top. Bake for 45 minutes at 350°F.

Appendix

State and Provincial Hunting Information

STATES

Alabama

Eastern cottontails and swamp rabbits inhabit the entire state, with some marsh rabbits in the extreme southeast and New England cottontails in the northeast sections of Alabama. Season dates were October 15–February 28, 1985. Department of Conservation and Natural Resources, Division of Game and Fish, 64 North Union Street, Montgomery, AL 36130 (205-832-6357).

Alaska

Alaska is home to both snowshoe and tundra hares, but snowshoes have the greatest distribution. Snowshoe hares are found over much of the state, according to Game Biologist Jeannette Ernest, with highest numbers usually present in the interior between the Alaska and Brooks mountain ranges. She said they are generally not found on the lower Kuskokwim delta, the Alaska Peninsula, and the area north of the Brooks Range. The Kenai Peninsula is experiencing very high snowshoe hare populations during 1985, according to Ernest.

According to Ernest, tundra hares are found primarily along the west coast of Alaska, including the Alaska Peninsula, with spotty distribution along the Arctic coast and the north slope of the Brooks Range. Tundra hares aren't considered an important game species because they are found in remote coastal areas of the state.

Hare hunting seasons during 1984–85 were September 1–April 30 in Units 1–5 and September 6–April 30 in Unit 14C. The daily bag limit was five in those units. There was no closed season and no bag limit in Units 6–26. Department of Fish

137

and Game, Box 3-2000, Juneau, AK 99802 (907-465-4190).

Arizona

The desert cottontail and black-tailed jack are the most common species in Arizona, distributed statewide. Eastern cottontails range across the center of the state into Mexico, and mountain cottontails reside in the northeast. The antelope jack, a species unique to deserts in the southcentral portion of the state, also call Arizona home. There is no closed season on rabbits and hare in Arizona. Game and Fish Department, 2222 West Greenway Rd., Phoenix, AZ 85023 (602-942-3000).

Arkansas

There are eastern cottontails, swamp rabbits, and black-tailed jacks in Arkansas; the first two are the most important to hunters. Both cottontails and swamp rabbits are distributed statewide, but swampers are found predominantly in bottomlands of the delta and coastal plain. Jacks occupy only the northwestern portion of the state, being most common in the Arkansas River valley, according to Small Game Biologist Rick Fowler.

Seasons usually run from the first week of October through February, with a daily bag limit of eight rabbits. Fowler said there are no rabbit harvest estimates for the state, but the average hunter success rate is .6 rabbit per hour. Game and Fish Commission, No. 2 Natural Resources Dr., Little Rock, AR 72205 (501-223-6346).

California

There are four types of rabbits and three species of hares in California. The desert cottontail inhabits much of the state, from Tehama County southward. Mountain cottontails occupy the north-east as well as some eastern counties in the middle of the state. Brush rabbits live all along the coast, extending farthest inland to the north; they also inhabit a band of brush country in the center of the state. Look for pygmy rabbits in sagebrush areas of Modoc, Lassen, and Mono counties.

Coniferous forests in northeastern California are home to snowshoe hares. Black-tailed jacks are distributed over most of the state in open grassland and semiopen brushland. White-tailed jacks are found along the east side of the Sierra Nevada and Cascade mountains from Tulare County to the Oregon border.

The 1984 season for rabbits and snowshoe hares in California was July 1–January 27, 1985. Daily bag limits were ten per day in Siskiyou, Shasta, Modoc, and Lassen counties and five a day in the remainder of the state. Jacks can be hunted all year, with no bag limit. Department of Fish and Game, 1416 Ninth St., Sacramento, CA 95814 (916-445-7613).

Colorado

Desert cottontails are distributed throughout Colorado, and mountain cottontails are found over all the state except the eastern end. Eastern cottontails are available to hunters in eastern Colorado, especially to the north. Snowshoe hares inhabit coniferous forests in mountains across the center of the state, with white-tailed jacks inhabiting most of the state and blacktails found primarily in the eastern half and southwest corner of the state.

Hunters can try for cottontails and snowshoes starting September 14, 1985, and the season usually extends to the end of February. Jacks are legal game all year. Division of Wildlife, 6060 Broadway, Denver, CO 80216 (303-297-1192).

Connecticut

There are eastern and New England cottontails, plus snowshoe and European hares in this state. Eastern cottontails are distributed statewide, with pockets of the New England variety scattered throughout the state, according to Small Game Biologist Peter Good. He said snowshoe hares are found primarily in the northwest, with some also in the northeast. Localized populations of European hares are in southwest Connecticut, according to Good.

The 1985–86 season dates for cottontails and European hares are October 19–December 7 and December 26–February 28, with daily bag limits of three rabbits and one hare. The bag limit on snowshoe hares is two per day during the season, which runs November 16–December 7 and December 26–January 31. Department of Environmental Protection, 165 Capitol Ave., Hartford, CT 06106 (203-566-4683).

Delaware

Delaware is home to the eastern cottontail. Wildlife Biologist Ken Reynolds says the population has been declining over the past ten years. During 1983, 9,950 hunters accounted for an estimated 57,426 cottontails in Delaware. The harvest was 109,558 by 15,814 hunters during 1974.

Season dates for 1984–85 were November 19–January 16 (January 13 in Newcastle County north of I-95) and January 21–26. The bag limit is four rabbits per day. Department of Natural Resources and Environmental Control, Division of Fish and Wildlife, 89 Kings Hwy., P.O. Box 1401, Dover, DE 19903 (302-736-5297).

Florida

The eastern cottontail and swamp rabbit are found throughout Florida, with cottontails generating most interest among hunters, according to Thomas Goodwin, Chief of the Bureau of Wildlife Resources. He said there are no closed seasons on rabbit hunting in the state. The daily bag limit is 12 and the possession limit 24. Game and Fresh Water Fish Commission, 620 South Meridian St., Tallahassee, FL 32301 (904-488-1960).

Georgia

Four types of rabbits are available in Georgia — eastern and New England cottontails, swamp and marsh rabbits. Easterns occupy the entire state. The New England variety is rare, found only in the north Georgia mountains, according to Wildlife Biologist Bob Monroe. He wrote that swamp rabbits inhabit the Piedmont, Ridge-Valley and upper coastal plain areas, while marsh rabbits are restricted to the coastal plain.

The annual harvest of rabbits is 575,664 by approximately 70,000 hunters, according to Monroe. Season dates were November 10, 1984–February 28, 1985. Department of Natural Resources, Game and Fish Division, 270 Washington St. S.W., Atlanta, GA 30334 (404-656-3530).

Hawaii

There are no rabbits native to Hawaii, but European domestics were released on some of the state's islands. They remain on Rabbit (Manana) Island near Oahu and Lehua Island, according to Wildlife Biologist Marie Morin. She said there is no hunting season open for rabbits on these islands because they are not abundant and the islands are seabird sanctuaries.

Idaho

Mountain and pygmy cottontails are the species hunters will encounter in Idaho, ranging across the southern half of the state, with pygmy rabbits isolated to the southern third. Snowshoe hares, white- and black-tailed jacks are also found here. Snowshoes and whitetails inhabit much of the state, while blacktails are primarily in southcentral and southwest Idaho.

Rabbits can be hunted September 1–February 28. An estimated 67,500 cottontails were harvested during 1983, compared to 156,800 during 1981. All hares, including jacks, can be hunted year-round. Department of Fish and Game, 600 S. Walnut, Box 25, Boise, ID 83707 (208-334-3700).

Illinois

The eastern cottontail provides a lot of hunter recreation statewide. Swamp rabbits may turn up in extreme southeast Illinois, and some white-tailed jacks may be seen in the northwest corner of the state. There were an estimated 1,320,940 rabbits bagged by 178,747 hunters here during the 1983 season. Season dates were November 10–January 6, 1985, with a bag limit of four bunnies. Department of Conservation, Lincoln Tower Plaza, 524 South Second Street, Springfield, IL 62706 (217-782-6384).

Indiana

Eastern cottontails range throughout Indiana, with swamp rabbits inhabiting swampy areas and wooded floodplains in the southwestern portions of the state. There were 600,000 rabbits bagged by an estimated 177,000 hunters in Indiana during the 1980–81 season. The statewide season for rabbits was November 9–January 31, 1985, with a daily bag limit of five. However, a number of designated public hunting areas were open to rabbit hunters starting October 1. Department of Natural Resources, Division of Fish and Wildlife, 607 State Office Bldg., Indianapolis, IN 46204 (317-232-4080).

Iowa

Eastern cottontails are found statewide in Iowa, with highest densities in the southern third of the state. White-tailed jacks occupy much of the state, except the southernmost and far eastern counties. Jacks are most common in the north.

The 1984–85 hunting season for cottontails was from September 1–February 28 and November 3–December 16 for jacks. There were 720,000 cottontails and 8,800 whitetails bagged during the 1983–84 season. Conservation Commission, Wallace State Office Bldg., Des Moines, IA 50319 (515-281-5918).

Kansas

Rabbits and hares can be hunted year-round in Kansas, with a daily bag limit of ten on cottontails and no limit on jack rabbits. From 778,000 to just over a million cottontails have been bagged by hunters in this state annually during recent years; hunter numbers have ranged from 77,500 to 92,500.

Eastern cottontails are found statewide wherever there is suitable cover. Desert cottontails inhabit the western third of Kansas. Swamp rabbits are restricted to extreme southeastern counties of Cherokee, Crawford, and Labette along the Neosho River and its tributaries.

Black-tailed jacks are the primary species of hare found in the state, distributed throughout, but most common in grasslands west of the Flint Hills. White-tailed jacks occasionally turn up in northwestern Kansas counties. Fish and Game Headquarters, Box 54A, Rural Rt. 2, Pratt, KS 67124.

Kentucky

Eastern cottontails and swamp rabbits are most common in Kentucky. There is also a record of a New England cottontail taken on Big Black Mountain in Harlan County, according to Technical Guidance Specialist Jimmy May. He said swamp rabbits are limited to wet areas in the western third of the state. The bluegrass section of central Kentucky consistently has the highest number of eastern cottontails, according to May.

The Kentucky rabbit season generally opens on the third Thursday in November and runs through January, with a daily bag limit of four rabbits. Over a million (1,118,500) rabbits were legally bagged by 140,500 hunters in Kentucky during the 1982–83 season. Department of Fish and Wildlife Resources, Frankfort, KY 40601 (502-564-4336).

Louisiana

Both eastern cottontails and swamp rabbits are found statewide in Louisiana, according to Upland Game Study Leader Mike Olinde. He wrote that a combined harvest of 200,000–250,000 is taken annually. Season dates for 1984–85 were October 1–February 28. Department of Wildlife and Fisheries, Game Division, P.O. Box 15570, Baton Rouge, LA 70895 (504-342-5868).

Maine

Maine is a stronghold for snowshoe hares—they occur statewide. Cottontails occupy only the southwestern corner of the state, south of Sebago Lake, according to Wildlife Biologist John Hunt. They are the New England species.

Hunting season dates have been October 1–March 31, with a daily bag limit of four hares or rabbits. The average annual harvest of snowshoes in the state from 1979 through 1983 was 262,564. Department of Inland Fisheries and Wildlife, 284 State St., State House Station 41, Augusta, ME 04333 (207-289-2871).

Maryland

Eastern and New England cottontails are the primary game species of rabbits in Maryland, according to Joshua Sandt, Upland Game Wildlife Program Manager. He said the eastern variety are found statewide, with highest populations in the Piedmont region. New England cottontails are found in the northeastern corner of Garrett County on Savage Mountain, where the habitat consists of northern hardwoods and evergreen trees.

Sandt said there are also black-tailed jacks inhabiting a nursery in Kent County on the Eastern Shore. The animals were introduced there around 1975 and have survived, but not expanded their range.

Rabbit season has been November 15–January 31, with a daily bag limit of six. Sandt said there are currently about 77,500 rabbit hunters in Maryland, and they harvest approximately 266,000 of the animals a year. Forest, Park and Wildlife Service, Towers State Office Bldg., Annapolis, MD 21401 (301-269-3195).

Massachusetts

Two types of cottontails, snowshoe hares and black-tailed jacks are found in this state. Jacks inhabit only Nantucket Island. Both eastern and New England cottontails are distributed statewide, with the eastern variety primarily inhabiting fields, farmland, and forest edges, while the New England variety is more fond of woodlands. Snowshoe hares prefer forested areas with a brushy understory.

Season dates have been October 20–

February 28 for cottontails, with the exception of Nantucket and Dukes counties, where the season opens November 15. Season openings are the same for snowshoe hares, but hunting ends for them on February 5 statewide.

There were 77,652 cottontails harvested by 23,212 hunters during 1979 in Massachusetts compared to a take of 150,213 bunnies by 31,748 hunters in 1977. The snowshoe hare harvest declined to 16,528 in 1979 from 27,620 in 1977 and 40,508 in 1968. Estimates of hunter numbers after hares are 15,967 for 1968; 9,932 in 1977; and 7,321 in 1979. Division of Fisheries and Wildlife, 100 Cambridge St., Boston, MA 02202 (617-727-3151).

Michigan

Eastern cottontails and snowshoe hares are the targets of Michigan rabbit hunters. Cottontails are most common in the southern third of the state, but are distributed throughout the Lower Peninsula and are found in conjunction with farmland and cities in the Upper Peninsula, primarily in Menominee, Delta, and Dickinson counties. The trend is just the opposite for snowshoe hares, with greatest numbers found in the Upper Peninsula and northern counties of the Lower Peninsula.

Season dates are September 15–March 31 statewide, with daily bag limits of five rabbits or hares. DNR spokesman Harry Hill said there were an estimated 852,980 cottontails harvested by 213,780 hunters during 1982 and 831,600 by 178,990 hunters during 1983. He said there were 313,210 snowshoe hares bagged by 79,210 hunters in 1982 and 177,060 hares taken by 59,860 hunters during 1983. Wildlife Division, Department of Natural Resources, Box 30028, Lansing, MI 48909 (517-373-1263).

Minnesota

Eastern cottontails, snowshoe hares, and white-tailed jacks are available to hunters in this state. Cottontails occur statewide, with best hunting in the southern half of Minnesota. Snowshoe hares are most abundant in the northern half. Jacks are distributed all along the western side, with their range extending across the southern third of the state.

Season dates for all three species during 1985–86 are September 14–February 28. There were 98,000 cottontails harvested during 1983 as opposed to 135,000 in 1982. Harvest figures for snowshoes were 21,000 during 1983 and 61,000 in 1982. Hunters bagged 13,000 and 27,000 jacks during 1983 and 1982. Department of Natural Resources, Division of Fish and Wildlife, Box 7, Centennial Office Bldg., 658 Cedar St., St. Paul, MN 55155 (612-296-6157).

Mississippi

Eastern cottontails and swamp rabbits are found throughout Mississippi. Season dates were October 15–February 28, 1985. Game and Fish Commission, P.O. Box 451, Jackson, MS 39205 (601-961-5300).

Missouri

Missouri has one of the highest annual harvests of eastern cottontails on record, with 2,300,117 taken by 204,782 hunters there during the 1982–83 season. More than two million cottontails were also bagged during 1981–82. These prolific rabbits are found statewide, with swamp rabbits inhabiting the southwest and southeast corners of the state. Black-tailed jacks occupy counties in the western third of Missouri.

Rabbits are legal game October 1–February 15, with a daily bag limit of six.

Department of Conservation, P.O. Box 180, Jefferson City, MO 65102 (314-751-4115).

Montana

Rabbit hunters have a free rein in Montana with year-round hunting and no bag limits. Eastern cottontails can be found along the eastern border of the state. Both mountain and desert cottontails are more common, with the desert variety in eastern counties and mountains throughout much of the state at low elevations. Pygmy rabbits have been reported only in the Grasshopper drainage in Beaverhead County.

Black-tailed jacks are confined to Beaverhead County, too. White-tailed jacks are common in open areas of the state. Snowshoe hares are common in forested areas of western Montana. Department of Fish, Wildlife and Parks, 1420 East Sixth Ave., Helena MT 59620 (406-444-2535).

Nebraska

Eastern and desert cottontails, plus white- and black-tailed jacks are available in Nebraska, according to Wildlife Biologist Frank Andelt. He said jacks are currently protected in the southeast portion of the state due to low populations. In the remainder of the state, blacktails are generally associated with cropland and whitetails with rangeland. The distribution of desert cottontails is limited to the western portion of Nebraska, while eastern cottontails are found statewide.

Season dates for all rabbits during 1984 were September 1–February 28, with a daily bag limit of seven on cottontails and eight on jacks. The area open to jack hunting is north and west of Nebraska 15 and U.S. 30. Game and Parks Commission, 2200 North 33rd St., P.O. Box 30370, Lincoln, NE 68503 (402-464-0641).

Nevada

Pygmy rabbits and two types of cottontails—mountain and desert—inhabit Nevada. Mountain rabbits are found over most of the state, pygmies are in the northern two-thirds, and the desert variety is distributed across the southern portion of the state. Nevada is also home to snowshoe hares (in west-central mountains), black-tailed jacks (statewide), and whitetails (northeast half, portion of northwest, and along most of western border).

Cottontails and pygmies could be hunted October 6–February 28, 1985 with a daily bag limit of ten. Jacks can be hunted at any time. Department of Wildlife, P.O. Box 10678, Reno, NV 89520 (702-784-6214).

New Hampshire

New England cottontails are the dominant species of rabbit in New Hampshire, inhabiting most of the state. Eastern cottontails can be found in the southern part. Snowshoe hares occur statewide.

Both rabbits and hares became legal game on October 1, 1984, with hunting for cottontails ending February 1, 1985, and hares legal through March 15. Fish and Game Department, 34 Bridge St., Concord, NH 03301 (603-271-3421).

New Jersey

New Jersey is generally a cottontail state, according to Robert Eriksen, Upland Game Project Leader; some European hares and black-tailed jacks, however, have been imported. He said hares and jacks are found in parts of Hunterdon, Somerset, Middlesex and Monmouth counties. Eastern cottontails are distributed statewide.

Rabbit and hare seasons were November 10–December 1 and December 10–February 9, 1985, with closures during gun deer hunts. The bag limits were four a day for cottontails and one a day for hares and jacks. Eriksen said there were an estimated 75,700 rabbit hunters during the 1983–84 season, who harvested 522,330 cottontails. Department of Environmental Protection, Division of Fish, Game and Wildlife, CN-400, Trenton, NJ 08625 (609-292-2965).

New Mexico
There are three species of jacks and two cottontails found in New Mexico. The jacks are blacktails, whitetails, and white-sided. The Animas and Playas valleys of Hidalgo County are the only locations in the United States where white-sided jacks are found. These rare animals are on the state's endangered species list, which gives them total protection. White-sided jacks are largely nocturnal and the front of their ears are tipped with black (on black-tailed jacks, ear tips are black on the back).

Eastern and mountain cottontails reside in New Mexico. All rabbits and hares, with the exception of white-sided jacks, can be hunted year-round and there is no bag limit. A small game or nongame hunting license is required. Department of Game and Fish, State Capitol, Sante Fe, NM 87503 (505-827-7882).

New York
Cottontails and snowshoe hares provide the bulk of the hunting opportunity in New York, but there are also European hares and black-tailed jacks in the state. There is a small colony of jacks, which were introduced, on the grounds of the Kennedy International Airport, according to Wildlife Biologist Ben Tullar.

He said that European hares were released at the village of Millbrook in Dutchess County around 1890. These hares can only be hunted in Dutchess, Putnam, and Westchester counties. The season was December 11–February 28, 1985, with a bag limit of one hare.

Eastern cottontails are distributed over most of the state, with some New England cottontails also found in the state. Total distribution of the New England variety isn't known, but they definitely inhabit the Rensselaer Hills east of the Hudson River, according to Tullar. Season dates for cottontails were October 1–February 28, 1985, in all but two of the state's southernmost counties, where the season opened November 1, 1984. The daily bag limit is six. There were 1,009,650 cottontails bagged by hunters in New York, according to the 1984 small game harvest survey.

Tullar said snowshoe hares are found in the Tug, Schohaire, and Showangunk hills, Helderberg and Neversink Highlands, plus the Adirondack, Catskill, and Taconic mountains. Season dates (October 1–March 17) are most liberal in the 14 northernmost counties, with a daily bag limit of six hares. Three other zones pictured in small game hunting regulation booklets have shorter seasons with daily bag limits of two. There were an estimated 146,282 snowshoes bagged in New York during the 1983–84 season. Department of Environmental Conservation, Fish and Wildlife Division, 50 Wolf Rd., Albany, NY 12233 (518-457-5400).

North Carolina
Eastern cottontails and marsh rabbits are the dominant species of bunnies in

North Carolina. Marsh rabbits inhabit wet habitat in the eastern half of the state, with easterns found statewide. There may be some New England cottontails along the western border of North Carolina. Dates for rabbit hunting were November 17, 1984 through February 28, 1985. Wildlife Resources Commission, 512 North Salisbury St., Raleigh, NC 27611 (919-733-3391).

North Dakota

Rabbits can be hunted year-round, with no bag limit in effect or license required, in North Dakota. White-tailed jacks are found statewide. Eastern cottontails reside in all but the southwestern portion of the state (Badlands), where they are replaced by desert cottontails, according to Upland Game Biologist Lowell Tripp. There are a few mountain cottontails in the western edge of the state. Tripp said snowshoe hares are present near the Canadian border along the eastern half of the state. Game and Fish Department, 2121 Lovett Ave., Bismarck, ND 58505 (701-224-2180).

Ohio

Cottontails are found throughout Ohio, with the animals most abundant in southeastern and eastern counties. Season dates were November 2–January 31, 1984, with a daily bag limit of four bunnies. There were 1,253,000 rabbits bagged in Ohio during the 1978–79 season, the latest year figures were provided, versus 2,816,000 taken during the 1972–73 season. Department of Natural Resources, Fountain Square, Columbus, OH 43224 (614-265-6789).

Oklahoma

Two species of rabbits and one of hares are found in Oklahoma—the eastern cottontail, swamp rabbit, and black-tailed jack. Cottontails and jacks are found statewide. Swamp rabbits are restricted to the eastern third of the state.

An estimated 115,290 hunters harvested 1,352,998 rabbits in Oklahoma during 1982, with a kill of 976,920 by 89,248 hunters during 1983. Season dates have been October 1–March 15. Department of Wildlife Conservation, 1801 North Lincoln, P.O. Box 53465, Oklahoma City, OK 73105 (405-521-3851).

Oregon

Rabbit hunters have it made in Oregon. There are no closed seasons or bag limits, plus there are a number of species available. Mountain cottontails, eastern cottontails, brush rabbits and pygmy rabbits live in this state. Species of hares include the snowshoe and white- and black-tailed jacks.

Mountain cottontails inhabit the mountains and sagebrush rangelands of eastern Oregon. The Willamette Valley is the primary stomping grounds of eastern cottontails. Brush rabbits inhabit heavy brush on the west side of the Cascade mountains. Dense sagebrush areas of southeast Oregon are homes for pygmy rabbits. Snowshoe hares are at home on timbered mountain slopes, and the jacks inhabit the desert or sagebrush plains of eastern and southeastern Oregon, plus the Willamette Valley. Department of Fish and Wildlife, P.O. Box 3503, Portland, OR 97208 (503-229-5551).

Pennsylvania

Both the eastern and New England cottontails enjoy wide distribution in Pennsylvania, with easterns found statewide and the New England variety in most of the state except the far west and part of the north, in forested habitat. Dale Sheffer, Bureau of Game Management Director, said there are also some snowshoe hares scattered across the northern third of Pennsylvania.

Season dates on snowshoes for 1984 were December 26–29, with a daily bag limit of two. Cottontails could be hunted November 3–24 and December 26–January 12, 1984, with four rabbits a day legal. Sheffer said approximately two thousand hares are harvested annually and close to two million cottontails. Game Commission, P.O. Box 1567, Harrisburg, PA 17105 (717-787-3633).

Rhode Island

There are both eastern and New England cottontails in Rhode Island, plus some snowshoe hares, according to Fish and Wildlife Spokesman Mark Saunders. The eastern variety is found statewide in suitable habitat, with New England cottontails found primarily in the northern and western part of the state. Hares occupy swamps and thick cover in western Rhode Island as well as in the vicinity of Tiverton and north of Little Compton.

Season dates for rabbits and hares have been October 20–December 7 and December 17–February 28. The daily bag limit is five for cottontails and two for hares. Department of Environmental Management, Division of Fish and Wildlife, Government Center, Tower Hill Rd., Wakefield, RI 02879 (401-789-3094).

South Carolina

Eastern cottontails are found throughout South Carolina. Swamp rabbits inhabit the Piedmont region, primarily adjacent to the Savannah River. The coastal plains are home to marsh rabbits.

There were an estimated 524,288 rabbits harvested by 46,955 hunters during the 1981-82 season. Season dates varied by zone, with November 22–March 1, 1985, being most common. Rabbit hunting was permitted year-round in some zones, with no bag limit. Other zones have daily bag limits of five rabbits. Wildlife Resources Department, P.O. Box 167, 1000 Assembly St., Columbia, SC 29202 (803-758-0001).

South Dakota

Eastern, mountain, and desert cottontails, plus white-tailed and black-tailed jacks are found in South Dakota. The eastern variety of cottontails is found statewide, except for parts of the Black Hills, according to Small Game Biologist Larry Fredrickson. He said mountain and desert cottontails inhabit the Black Hills. The desert variety also occupies the northwestern portion of South Dakota.

White-tailed jacks occur statewide, and the blacktails are in the southcentral counties, according to Fredrickson. The 1984-85 season on cottontails was October 1–February 28, with a daily bag limit of ten. Jacks can be taken year-round. There were an estimated 103,900 cottontails harvested in South Dakota during the 1982–83 season and 129,300 bagged during the 1983–84 hunt, according to Fredrickson. Department of Game, Fish and Parks, Anderson Bldg., Pierre, SD 57501 (605-773-3485).

Tennessee

Tennessee's rabbit hunters will find eastern cottontails statewide and the New England variety in the eastern third of the state. Some snowshoe hares reside in the mountainous northeast, too. Swamp rabbits occur in western Tennessee. Season dates for all species were November 10–February 28, 1985, with a daily bag limit

of five. Wildlife Resources Agency, P.O.
Box 40747, Nashville, TN 37204 (615-360-
0621).

Texas

There are four species of cottontails in
Texas—eastern, mountain, Davis Mountains, and swamp—according to Don
Wilson, Upland Game Program Leader.
Easterns are found over most of the state,
with the exception of far western counties.
Davis Mountains cottontails are thought
by some to be simply a subspecies of the
eastern cottontail. At any rate, they are
found primarily in the pinion-oak-juniper
woodlands of the Chisos, Chinati, Davis,
and Guadalupe mountains of Jeff Davis,
Culberson, Presidio, and Brewster counties. The swamp species lives in suitable
habitat in the eastern third of Texas.

The black-tailed jack, the only hare in
the state, occupies much of the state, being
absent from a band of counties in eastern
Texas. Rabbits can be hunted at any time
in Texas and there is no bag limit, according to Wilson. He said an estimated
1,070,513 rabbits were harvested by
183,108 hunters during 1982 and early
1983. Parks and Wildlife Department,
4200 Smith School Rd., Austin, TX 78744
(512-479-4800).

Utah

Utah has three species each of rabbits
and hares: desert, mountain, and pygmy
rabbits, and snowshoes, white-tailed and
black-tailed jacks. Cottontails and jack
rabbits are distributed statewide, with
snowshoes occupying coniferous forests in
mountainous areas.

Season dates for cottontails and snowshoes for 1984-85 were either September
15 or 17–January 31, with daily bag limits
of five for hares and five or ten for cotton-

tails, depending on the county hunted.
There is no closed season, bag limit, or
license required for hunting jacks. An
estimated 156,696 cottontails were collected by 26,714 hunters during 1982, and
22,467 hunters harvested 180,767 during
1983. The harvests on snowshoe hares
during 1982 and 1983 were 9,257 and
6,302 by 4,245 and 3,544 hunters respec-
tively. Wildlife Resources, 1596 West
North Temple, Salt Lake City, UT 84116
(801-533-9333).

Vermont

Snowshoe hares and cottontails are
present in Vermont. Both eastern and New
England cottontails are found here, but
the eastern species is considered most
abundant. Best cottontail concentrations
are found in the lower Connecticut River
Valley and the southwestern quarter of the
state (west of the Green Mountain range
and up the Champlain Valley to the Canadian border), according to John Hall,
Director of Game and Education. He said
that the northern third of the state has the
greatest amount of hare habitat, but
snowshoes are also available in the Green
Mountain range.

Rabbit and hare hunting seasons begin
the fourth Saturday in September in Vermont and extend through the second Sun-
day in March. The daily bag limit is three
rabbits or hares, singly or in combination.
Fish and Game Department, Montpelier,
VT 05602 (802-828-3371).

Virginia

Eastern and New England cottontails
inhabit this state, with easterns found
statewide and the New England species
found in mountain counties in the west
and northwestern portions of the state.
New England cottontails are generally

located at elevations greater than 2,000 feet, according to Research Biologist Dennis Martin. He said there are also two or three small remnant populations of snowshoe hares in mountain counties.

Rabbit hunting begins on the first Monday in November over most of the state. Accomack and Northampton counties open on the second Monday of the month. The season ends January 31 statewide, and the daily bag limit is six rabbits. Commission of Game and Inland Fisheries, 4010 West Broad St., P.O. Box 11104, Richmond, VA 23230 (804-257-1000).

Washington

Snowshoe hares are the most abundant and widespread member of the rabbit family in Washington. There are few places in the state where they aren't found. The only species of rabbit is the mountain cottontail; they are found across the eastern half of Washington, as are white-tailed jacks. A small portion of the southeast contains some black-tailed jacks.

Dates during a recent season on cottontails and snowshoes were October 13–February 28 in eastern Washington and September 1–February 28 in the west. Department of Game, 600 Capitol Way, Olympia, WA 98504 (206-753-5700).

West Virginia

Either eastern or New England cottontails are found in every county of this state. The New England species is most often found in wooded, mountainous habitat. Some snowshoe hares are found in the Allegheny Mountains in the eastern part of the state.

Season dates for rabbits and hares were November 3–February 28, 1985. There were an estimated 484,034 rabbits bagged by 114,768 hunters in West Virginia during the 1980 season. Department of Natural Resources, 1800 Washington St. East, Charleston, WV 25305 (304-348-2754).

Wisconsin

There are eastern cottontails, snowshoe hares, and some white-tailed jacks in Wisconsin. Cottontails are distributed statewide, with the best hunting in the southern two-thirds of the state. Snowshoes occupy the northern two-thirds of Wisconsin, with jacks showing up along the western border.

Season dates for cottontails in the northern half of the state were September 15–February 28, 1985, starting October 20 (at noon) in the southern portion of the state. The boundary between north and south zones is along Highway 54 between Algoma and Waupaca and along Highway 10 from Waupaca to Prescott. Jacks could be hunted from October 20 (at noon) to November 5, 1984. The daily bag limit for cottontails and jacks is three. There is no closed season or bag limit on snowshoe hares in Wisconsin. Department of Natural Resources, Bureau of Wildlife Management, Box 7921, Madison, WI 53707 (608-266-1877).

Wyoming

Cottontails are found throughout Wyoming, according to Information Manager Al Langston, with the mountain species everywhere except the southeast. Eastern cottontails occupy the southeast. Desert cottontails are found in prairie or desert habitat where it occurs. Snowshoe hares inhabit the state's coniferous forests. White-tailed and black-tailed jacks are widely distributed in the state.

The 1984 season on cottontails and snowshoe hares was September 1–Februcommand ary 28. There were 462,837 cottontails harvested in Wyoming during 1983 and 3,563 snowshoes, according to Langston. Best counties for cottontails are Natrona, Carbon and Sweetwater. Jacks are classified as predators and can be hunted any time without a license. Game and Fish Department, Cheyenne, WY 82002 (307-777-7735).

CANADIAN PROVINCES

Alberta

Alberta is home to snowshoe hares, white-tailed jacks, and eastern cottontails. Snowshoes are distributed provincewide; jacks and cottontails are confined to the southern portion. Rabbits and hares can be hunted year-round. Energy and Natural Resources, Fish and Wildlife Division, 9945 108th St., Edmonton, Alberta T5K 2C9 (403-427-8580).

British Columbia

Snowshoe hares are available throughout this province. Eastern cottontails have been introduced to the Lower Mainland and Vancouver Island. Both of these species can be hunted all year. White-tailed jacks and mountain cottontails, on the other hand, are totally protected in the Okanagan Valley, the only part of the province where they occur. Ministry of Environment, Fish and Wildlife Branch, Parliament Bldgs., Victoria, British Columbia V8V 1X5 (604-387-4573).

Manitoba

Snowshoe hares are most common here, distributed throughout the province. White-tailed jacks can be found south of Lake Winnipeg, along with the eastern cottontail. The northeastern section of Manitoba is home to Arctic hares. Rabbits and hares are not protected in the province, meaning they can be hunted any time, including Sundays. Call 204-945-6784 for hunting information. Department of Mines, Natural Resources and Environment, Box 24, 1495 St. James St., Winnipeg, Manitoba R3H 0W9.

New Brunswick

Snowshoe hares are found throughout this province, according to Wildlife Biologist David Cartwright. He said they can be hunted, live-trapped, or snared from October 1 to the end of February. There is no bag limit. Department of Natural Resources, Fish and Wildlife Branch, P.O. Box 6000, Fredericton, New Brunswick E3B 5H1 (506-453-2433).

Newfoundland/Labrador

Snowshoe and Arctic hares occupy this province, but the larger Arctic variety is rare on much of the island of Newfoundland. These hares are being reintroduced to parts of the island in an effort to increase their numbers. Arctic hares are presently found in the Northern and Southern Long Range Mountains, on the Buchans Plateau, and Brunette Island of Newfoundland. These hares are found all along the eastern portion of Labrador, with their range extending farthest inland in the center of the mainland.

Snowshoe hares are not native to Newfoundland; they were introduced there from Nova Scotia between 1864 and 1876. Snowshoe hare numbers are highest in the interiors of Newfoundland and Labrador.

Both hunting and snaring hares is legal in this province. Arctic hares cannot be hunted on Newfoundland. During a recent season snowshoe hares could be hunted October 1–March 12 on the eastern

Avalon Peninsula and the Bonavista Peninsula. Snowshoes were legal only October 1–December 31 on the rest of the island. Both Arctic and snowshoe hares could be hunted October 1–March 31 during a recent season in Labrador. Department of Culture, Recreation and Youth, Wildlife Division, Bldg. 810, Pleasantville, St. Johns, Newfoundland A1C 5T7 (709-737-2815).

Northwest Territories

Snowshoe hares inhabit much of the Northwest Territories where there are coniferous forests. Arctic hares are distributed north and east of Great Slave Lake. There was no closed season for taking hares here during 1985. Department of Renewable Resources, Box 2668, Yellowknife, Northwest Territories, X1A 2L9 (403-920-8043).

Nova Scotia

Snowshoe hares get all the attention of rabbit hunters in Nova Scotia, being common provincewide. Dates for hunting hares in this province are November 16–February 28, with no bag limit. There were 508,124 hares harvested by 27,959 hunters during the 1983–84 season, according to Upland Game Biologist Neil Van Nostrand. Department of Land and Forests, P.O. Box 698, Halifax, Nova Scotia B3J 2T9 (902-424-4297).

Ontario

There is one species of rabbit and two of hares available to hunters in Ontario — eastern cottontails and snowshoe and European hares. Cottontails and European hares are restricted to the southern portion of the province between the Great Lakes of Huron, Ontario, and Erie on into Quebec where farmland and brushy cover provide suitable habitat. Snowshoe hares are distributed throughout most of the province where swamps and stands of evergreen trees provide adequate cover.

European hares were introduced to Ontario during 1912 when nine of the animals from Germany gained their freedom near Brantford. They flourished in their new home and now are an important small game species in parts of the province. Information on best locations to hunt these hares can be obtained from Ministry of Natural Resources offices at Owen Sound, Simcoe, Aylmer, Wingham, Cambridge, and Huronia.

Besides the species mentioned above, another hare — the white-tailed jack — occasionally shows up in the Rainy River region near the Manitoba border. Season dates for 1984-85 in Ontario varied considerably, depending on management unit. The most liberal season was September 1–June 15, which was in effect for most of the province. However, season dates were October 31–February 28 in units 93 and 94. Daily bag limits were six for each species of rabbit, although there was no bag limit for snowshoe hares in some units.

Ministry of Natural Resources spokesman Charlie Ross said there were 215,000 cottontails harvested by 44,000 hunters during 1980; 271,000 snowshoe hares were bagged by 43,600 hunters; and 45,500 European hares were collected by 18,400 hunters. Ministry of Natural Resources, Outdoor Recreation, Wildlife Branch, Parliament Bldg., Toronto, Ontario M7A 1W3 (416-965-4251).

Prince Edward Island

Snowshoe hares are available on this small island province. Hare populations are consistently good on the island, ac-

cording to Wildlife Biologist Alan Godfrey. Also of interest is that the incidence
of melanistic (black) hares is higher here
than elsewhere. Godfrey wrote that some
years, 1 percent of the hares harvested on
the island are melanistic.

The 1984–85 season for snowshoes here
was November 1–February 28, with a
daily bag limit of five. Hares can also be
legally snared. The total estimated harvest
of hares on Prince Edward Island during
1983–84 was 22,510 by 2,065 hunters. Fish
and Wildlife Division, Department of
Community Affairs, P.O. Box 2000,
Charlottetown, Prince Edward Island
(902-892-0311).

Quebec

Both snowshoe and Arctic hares inhabit
this province, with snowshoes inhabiting
all but the Ungava Peninsula and Arctic
hares most common on that peninsula.
The range of Arctic hares extends south of
the peninsula, so there is some overlap
between the two species of hares. Eastern
cottontails occur in the extreme southern
portion of Quebec.

The 1985 season dates for hunting hares
and rabbits are September 21–March 1
over much of the province. In zones 23
and 24 the dates are August 25–April 30,
with opening dates of September 1 in zone
22 and September 14 in zone 19. Snaring
rabbits and hares is also legal in the province during specified seasons. Department
of Tourism, Fish and Game, 150 St.
Cyrille E., Quebec City, Quebec G1R 4Y1
(418-643-2464).

Saskatchewan

The two types of rabbits occupying this
province — eastern and mountain — are
restricted to the southwest corner, with
mountains having the largest range. Two
hares — snowshoe and white-tailed jacks —
live in Saskatchewan, too. Highest numbers of snowshoes are available in the
northern two-thirds of the province, and
white-tailed jacks in the southern third
(from Prince Albert southward). Rabbits
and hares are not protected at any time in
the province. Parks and Renewable Resources, 3211 Albert St., Regina, Saskatchewan S4S 5W6.

Yukon Territory

Snowshoe hares can be hunted in the
Yukon year-round, with the exception of
Management Unit 6, which is closed to
hunting. These hares are found provincewide. Department of Renewable Resources, Wildlife Branch, Box 2703,
Whitehorse, Yukon Territory Y1A 2C6
(403-667-5221).

Additional Reading

Brakefield, Tom. *The Sportsman's Complete Book of Trophy and Meat Care*. Harrisburg, Pennsylvania: Stackpole Books, 1975.

———— *Small Game Hunting*. Philadelphia: J. B. Lippincott Co., 1978.

Bryant, John P. "Hare Trigger." *Natural History*. November 1981, 46–53.

Grange, Wallace Byron. *The Way to Game Abundance*. New York: Charles Scribner's Sons, 1949.

LaBarbera, Mark. "Tracking Harey Houdinis." *North American Hunter*. Jan./Feb. 1985.

Mueller, Larry, "Return of the Real Rabbit Dog." *Outdoor Life*. March 1983, 86–87.

Pearce, Michael. "Up Your Cottontail Score." *Outdoor Life*. December 1982, 54–55.

Rue, Leonard Lee. *Cottontails*. New York: Crowell Co., 1965.

Smith, Todd. "1984–85 Hunting Seasons." *Petersen's Hunting, 1985 Annual*. Los Angeles, 1984.

Tinsley, Russell, ed. *All About Small Game Hunting in America*. Piscataway, New Jersey: Winchester Press, 1976.

Trueblood, Ted. "The Great Rabbit Roundup." *Field and Stream*. April 1982, 11, 14–16.

Whitaker, Jr., John O. *The Audubon Society Field Guide to North American Mammals*. New York: Alfred A. Knopf, 1980.

Williams, Ted. "Yankee Cottontails." *Audubon*. September 1983, 18–23.

Zumbo, Jim. "Rocky Mountain Rabbits." *American Hunter*. November 1984, 27, 54.

Index

Note: Italic numbers refer to tables